Christmas 1979

nearly an island

NEARLY AN ISLAND

a Nova Scotian anthology

edited by
Alice Hale
Sheila Brooks

BREAKWATER BOOKS LIMITED

© Copyright 1979, Breakwater Books Limited.

Published by Breakwater Books Limited
277 Duckworth Street
St. John's, Newfoundland
A1C 1G9

Canadian Cataloguing in Publication Data

Main entry under title:

Nearly an island

ISBN 0-919948-65-0 bd.   ISBN 0-919948-64-2 pa.

1. Nova Scotia — Literary collections.
2. Canadian literature (English) — Nova Scotia.*
I. Hale, Alice K., 1937-   II. Brooks,
Sheila A., 1937-

PS8255.N6N43   C810'8'032   C79-094208-9
PR9198.2.N6N43

Printed by
ROBINSON-BLACKMORE LTD.
St. John's, Newfoundland, Canada.

To our Canadian Literature students

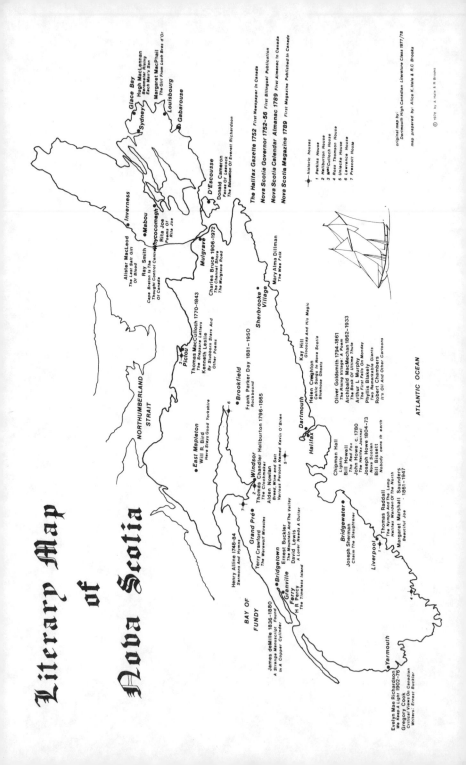

Literary Map of Nova Scotia

Glace Bay
Hugh MacLennan
Barometer Rising
Each Man's Son

Margaret MacPhail
The Girl From Loch Bras d'Or

Sydney
Louisbourg
Gabarouse

Inverness
Alister MacLeod
The Lost Salt Gift Of Blood

Mabou
Ray Smith
Cape Breton Is The Thought Control Centre Of Canada

Whycocomagh
Rita Joe
Poems Of Rita Joe

D'Escousse
Donald Cameron
Faces Of Leacock
The Education Of Everett Richardson

The Halifax Gazette 1752 *First Newspaper In Canada*

Nova Scotia Governor 1752-56 *First Bilingual Publication*

Nova Scotia Calendar Almanac 1789 *First Almanac In Canada*

Nova Scotia Magazine 1789 *First Magazine Published In Canada*

Mulgrave
Charles Bruce 1906-1972
The Channel Shore
The Mulgrave Road

Mary Alma Dillman
The Wee Folk

Pictou
Thomas MacCulloch 1770-1843
The Stepsure Letters

Kenneth Leslie
By Stubborn Stars And Other Poems

Sherbrooke Village

East Maitland
Will R. Bird
Here Stays Good Yorkshire

Brookfield
Frank Parker Day 1881-1950
Rockbound

Windsor
Thomas Chandler Haliburton 1796-1865
The Clockmaker

Alden Nowlan
Bread, Wine and Salt
Various Persons Named Kevin O'Brien

Kay Hill
Glooscap And His Magic

Helen Creighton
Celtic Songs In Nova Scotia
Bluenose Ghosts

Oliver Goldsmith 1794-1861
The Rising Village: A Poem

Archibald MacMechan 1862-1933
The Book Of Ultima Thule

Arthur L. Murphy
The Halifax Journal

Phyllis Blakely
Two Remarkable Giants

Robert Chambers
It's Oil And Other Cartoons

Dartmouth

Halifax
Chipman Hall
Lightly

Bill Howell
The Red Fox

John Howe, c. 1780
The Halifax Journal

Joseph Howe 1804-73
Poems and Essays

Bill Bissett
Nobody owns th earth

Grand Pré
Henry Alline 1748-84
Sermons And Hymns

Terry Crawford
The Werewolf Miracles

Bridgetown
Ernest Buckler
The Mountain And The Valley

David Lewis
A Lover Needs A Guitar

Granville Ferry
H R Percy
The Timeless Island

James deMille 1836-1880
A Strange Manuscript Found In A Copper Cylinder

Bridgewater
Joseph Sherman
Chaim The Slaughterer

Liverpool
Thomas Raddall
The Nymph And The Lamp
Halifax Warden Of The North

Margaret Marshall Saunders 1861-1947
Beautiful Joe

Yarmouth
Evelyn Mae Richardson
We Keep A Light 1902-76

Gregory Cook
Critical Views On Canadian Writers: Ernest Buckler

NORTHUMBERLAND STRAIT

BAY OF FUNDY

ATLANTIC OCEAN

↑ = historic houses

1 Perkins House
2 Haliburton House
3 McCulloch House
4 Ross Thomson House
5 Uniacke House
6 Lawrence House
7 Prescott House

© 1978 by A Hale & B Brooks

original map by:
Dartmouth High Canadian Literature Class 1977/78

map prepared by: Alice K Hale & R C Brooks

Note on the illustrations:

Five of the illustrations included in this collection are Micmac petroglyphs — rock engravings — found at Lake Kejimkoojik and Medway River. These petroglyphs were carved with sharp arrowheads, pieces of quartz or even a sharpened tip of bone or antler. They are the record of what the Micmac wished to preserve.

Front cover — petroglyph found at Medway. A small boat with figures, one at tiller. The drawing is reduced in size from the original petroglyph. It is an Indian's impression of a small boat something like a shallop; shallops or longboats were used to land a party on shore.

"Before the coming of the white man an Indian girl dreamed that a small island floated in toward the land. On the island were bare trees and men — one dressed in garments of white rabbit skins. She told her dream to the wise men but they could not explain the meaning. The next day at dawn, the Indians saw, as the girl had dreamed, a small island near the shore. There were trees on the island and bears, as the Indians supposed, climbing among the bare branches of the trees. They seized their bows and arrows to shoot the bears. To their amazement the bears were men, some of them lowering into the water a strange canoe into which they jumped and paddled ashore. Among the men was one dressed in a white robe who came toward them making signs of peace and good will and, raising his hand, pointed toward the heavens. The white man and the white man's ways had come to the land of the Micmacs."

Back cover — This petroglyph depicts a village consisting of houses without chimneys.*

The remaining drawings are visualizations of Ernest Buckler quotations. Buckler gives us a uniquely Nova Scotian world view and artist Albert Moskowitz translates his message into a concrete image.

*Rock Drawings of the Micmac Indians, Marion Robertson. The Nova Scotia Museum. Halifax, NS., 1973.

TABLE OF CONTENTS

INTRODUCTION

"Nova Scotia is nearly an island . . ." an image that captures the essence of our singularity. It describes us both physically and psychologically. Predominant in our literature is a sense of place, the emotional pull of land and sea. Rather than a merely parochial attachment, our "arteries go out to the Main." We are bound to our historical context. But even stronger are our ties to humanity. The authors in this anthology reveal a remarkable awareness of setting. In almost every selection, however, the emphasis is upon the people in that setting. Characteristically, they are described with sensitivity and gentleness and a touch of sadness.

Nova Scotians pride themselves on having a long history, both cultural and political. Puritans settled the farms left vacant by the Expulsion of the Acadians; Loyalists came after the American Revolution; 40,000 Scots arrived after 1815. But first generation settlers were usually too busy to write. A few, Jonathan Odell and Joseph Stansbury, wrote patriotic songs and nostalgic lyrics of their homeland. Henry Alline, an itinerant evangelist, wrote prayers and sermons to save the souls of Nova Scotians.

A literary community developed in Nova Scotia at least a generation earlier than in Upper and Lower Canada. By the 1820's a cultural environment — schools, colleges, museums, libraries, theatres — existed to stimulate young writers. Joseph

Howe, Thomas McCulloch, Thomas Chandler Haliburton and Oliver Goldsmith were the first wave of native authors. While Howe fostered in us a spirit of political independence, McCulloch and Haliburton laughed at our foibles and "slow ways". Goldsmith's "The Rising Village" idealized the growth of a Loyalist settlement.

Through the years our province has been associated in the minds of others with the Bluenose, the Great Explosion, Halifax Harbour in World War II, fishing villages, coal mines, and Evangeline. However much these associations have become stereotypes, they are also real — tangibles in our past which have helped to form our souls. Charles Bruce's *Channel Shore*, Frank Parker Day's *Rockbound*, Hugh MacLennan's *Each Man's Son*, Ernest Buckler's *The Mountain and the Valley*, and Thomas Raddall's *Halifax, Warden of the North* capture the past of Nova Scotia and a way of life many of us romanticize.

Even yet the focus remains more rural than urban. Perhaps this vision of our dependence on the natural environment accounts for the continuing predominance of male characters.

Thus another generation of writers looks anew at many of the same themes and images. *The Education of Everett Richardson* by Silver Donald Cameron introduces readers to another view of those who man the fishing boats — the little men in conflict with forces almost as strong as the sea itself. Alden Nowlan's stories and poetry make poverty and despair something which man can live through but not always conquer. The poetry of a young Maxine Tynes or Joe Sherman beside that of Charles Bruce carries the line on and on...

Two books combine the artistic imagery of poet, prose writer, photographer, and painter to give an interpretation of the land and sea which makes the reader feel the texture of this region. *Shaped By The Land* (poetry by Alden Nowlan and paintings by Tom Forrestall and *Window on the Sea* (text by Ernest Buckler and photographs by Hans Weber) capture these two constants of land and sea in our past and present.

This anthology is obviously not an historical or chronological collection; nor is it primarily thematic. Rather, it reflects the tastes of two people who have found in our literature interwoven patterns of time and place. It is an attempt to reveal the blood and spirit of what has been written by Bluenosers who have done something else besides "eat, drink, smoke, sleep, ride about, lounge at taverns, make speeches at temperance meetin's, and talk about 'House of Assembly'." (*The Clockmaker*, Haliburton.)

Nova Scotia is nearly an island,
nearly the last place left
where place and people
are not thinned and adulterated
with graftings that grow across the grain.
Yet what saves it from insularity
is a peninsularity like that of the heart.
The arteries go out to the main,
but the beat is all of itself.
Sometimes it seems self-contradictory.
It is grounded in the sea,
but rooted in the land.
Its features are as varied
as those of the body.

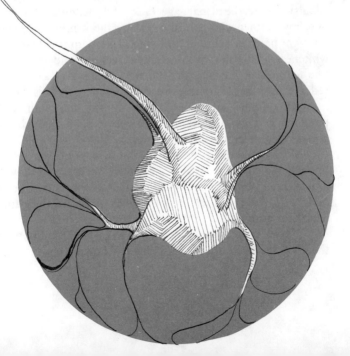

The Return

Alistair MacLeod

It is an evening during the summer that I am ten years old and I am on a train with my parents as it rushes toward the end of eastern Nova Scotia. "You'll be able to see it any minute now, Alex," says my father excitedly, "look out the window, any minute now."

He is standing in the aisle by this time with his left hand against the overhead baggage rack while leaning over me and over my mother who is in the seat by the window. He grasped my right hand in his right and when I look up it is first into the whiteness of his shirt front arching over me and then into the fine features of his face, the blueness of his eyes and his wavy reddish hair. He is very tall and athletic looking. He is forty-five.

"Oh Angus, sit down," says my mother with mingled patience and exasperation, "he'll see it soon enough. We're almost there. Please sit down; people are looking at you."

My left hand lies beside my mother's right on the green upholstered cushion. My mother has brown eyes and brown hair and is three years younger than my father. She is very beautiful and her picture is often in the society pages of the papers in Montreal which is where we live.

"There it is," shouts my father triumphantly. "Look Alex, there's Cape Breton!" He takes his left down from the baggage rack and points across us to the blueness that is the Strait of Canso, with the gulls hanging almost stationary above the tiny fishing boats and the dark green of the spruce and fir mountains rising out of the water and trailing white wisps of mist about them like discarded ribbons hanging about a newly opened package.

The train lurches and he almost loses his balance and quickly has to replace his hand on the baggage rack. He is sqeezing my right hand so hard he is hurting me and I can feel my fingers going numb within his grip. I would like to mention it but I do not know how to do so politely and I know he does not mean to cause me pain.

"Yes, there it is," says my mother without much enthusiasm, "now you can sit down like everybody else."

He does so but continues to hold my hand very fiercely. "Here," says my mother not unkindly, and passes him a Kleenex over my head. He takes it quietly and I am reminded of the violin records which he has at home in Montreal. My mother does not like them and says they all sound the same so he only plays them when she is out and we are alone. Then it is a time like church, very solemn and serious and sad and I am not supposed to talk but I do not know what else I am supposed to do; especially when my father cries.

Now the train is getting ready to go across the water on a boat. My father releases my hand and starts gathering our luggage because we are to change trains on the other side. After this is done we all go out on the deck of the ferry and watch the Strait as we groan over its placid surface and churn its tranquillity into the roiling turmoil of our own white-watered wake.

My father goes back into the train and reappears with the cheese sandwich which I did not eat and then we go to the stern of the ferry where the other people are tossing food to the convoy of screaming gulls which follows us on our way. The gulls are the whitest things that I have ever seen; whiter than the sheets on my bed at home, or the pink-eyed rabbit that died, or the winter's first snow. I think that since they are so beautiful they should somehow have more manners and in some way be more refined. There is one mottled brown, who feels very ill at ease and flies low and to the left of the noisy main flock. When he ventures into the thick of the fray his fellows scream and peck at him and drive him away. All three of us try to toss our pieces of cheese sandwich to him or into the water directly before him. He is so lonesome and all alone.

When we get to the other side we change trains. A blond young man is hanging from a slowly chugging train with one hand and drinking from a bottle which he holds in the other. I think it is a very fine idea and ask my father to buy me some pop. He says he will later but is strangely embarrassed. As we cross the tracks to our train, the blond young man begins to sing: "There once was an Indian maid." It is not the nice version but the dirty one which I and my friends have learned from the bigger boys in the sixth grade. I have somehow never before thought of grown-ups singing it. My parents are now walking very fast, practically dragging me by the hand over the troublesome tracks. They are both very red-faced and we all pretend we do not hear the voice that is receding in the distance.

When we are seated on the new train I see that my mother is very angry. "Ten years," she snaps at my father, "ten years I've raised this child in the city of Montreal and he has never seen an adult drink liquor out of a bottle, nor heard that kind of language. We have not been here five minutes and that is the first thing he sees and hears." She is on the verge of tears.

"Take it easy, Mary," says my father soothingly. "He doesn't understand. It's all right."

"It's not all right," says my mother passionately. "It's not all right at all. It's dirty and filthy and I must have been out of my mind to agree to this trip. I wish we were going back tomorrow."

The train starts to move and before long we are rattling along the shore. There are fishermen in little boats who wave

14

good-naturedly at the train and I wave back. Later there are the black gashes of coal mines which look like scabs upon the greenness of the hills and the blueness of the ocean and I wonder if these are the mines in which my relatives work.

This train goes much slower than the last one and seems to stop every five minutes. Some of the people around us are talking in a language that I know is Gaelic although I do not understand it, others are sprawled out in their seats, some of them drowsing with their feet stuck out in the aisle. At the far end of the aisle two empty bottles roll endlessly back and forth clinking against themselves and the steel-bottomed seats. The coach creaks and sways.

The station is small and brown. There is a wooden platform in front of it illuminated by lights which shine down from two tall poles and are bombarded by squads of suicidal moths and June bugs. Beneath the lights there are little clusters of darkly clad men who talk and chew tobacco, and some ragged boys about my own age who lean against battered bicycles waiting for the bundles of newspapers that thud on the platform before their feet.

Two tall men detach themselves from one of the groups and approach us. I know they are both my uncles although I have only seen the younger one before. He lived at our house during part of the year that was the first grade and used to wrestle with me on the floor and play the violin records when no one was in. Then one day he was gone forever to survive only in my mother's neutral "It was the year your brother was here," or the more pointed "It was the year your drunken brother was here."

Now both men are very polite. They shake hands with my father and say "Hello Angie" and then, taking off their caps, "How do you do" to my mother. Then each of them lifts me up in the air. The younger one asks me if I remember him and I say "Yes" and he laughs, and puts me down. They carry our suitcases to a taxi and then we all bounce along a very rough street and up a hill, bump, bump, and stop before a large dark house which we enter.

In the kitchen of the house there are a great many people sitting around a big coal-burning stove even though it is summer. They all get up when we come in and shake hands and the women put their arms around my mother. Then I am introduced to the grandparents I have never seen. My grandmother is very tall with hair almost as white as the afternoon's gulls and eyes like the sea over which they flew. She wears a long black dress with a blue checkered apron over it and lifts me off my feet in powerful hands so that I can kiss her and look into her eyes. She smells of soap and water and hot rolls and asks me how I like living in Montreal. I have never lived anywhere else so I say I guess it is all right.

My grandfather is short and stocky with heavy arms and very big hands. He has brown eyes and his once red hair is almost all white now except for his eyebrows and the hair of his nostrils. He has a white moustache which reminds me of the walrus picture at school and the bottom of it is stained brown by the tobacco that he is chewing even now and spitting the juice into a coal scuttle which he keeps beside his chair. He is wearing a blue plaid shirt and brown trousers supported by heavy suspenders. He too lifts me up although he does not kiss me and he smells of soap and water and tobacco and leather. He asks me if I saw any girls that I liked on the train. I say "No," and he laughs and lowers me to the floor.

And now it is later and the conversation has died down and the people have gradually filtered out into the night until there are just the three of us, and my grandparents, and after a while my grandmother and my mother go upstairs to finalize the sleeping arrangements. My grandfather puts rum and hot water and sugar into two glasses and gives one to my father and then allows me to sit on his lap even though I am ten, and gives me sips from his glass. He is very different from Grandpa Gilbert in

Montreal who wears white shirts and dark suits with a vest and a gold watch-chain across the front.

"You have been a long time coming home," he says to my father. "If you had come through that door as often as I've thought of you I'd've replaced the hinges a good many times."

"I know, I've tried, I've wanted to, but it's different in Montreal you know."

"Yes I guess so. I just never figured it would be like this. It seems so far away and we get old so quickly and a man always feels a certain way about his oldest son. I guess in some ways it is a good thing that we do not all go to school. I could never see myself being owned by my woman's family."

"Please don't start that already," says my father a little angrily. "I am not owned by anybody and you know it. I am a lawyer and I am in partnership with another lawyer who just happens to be my father-in-law. That's all."

"Yes, that's all," says my grandfather and gives me another sip from his glass. "Well, to change the subject, is this the only one you have after being married eleven years?"

My father is now red-faced like he was when we heard the young man singing. He says heatedly: "You know you're not changing the subject at all. I know what you're getting at. I know what you mean."

"Do you?" asks my grandfather quietly. "I thought perhaps that was different in Montreal too."

The two women come downstairs just as I am having another sip from the glass. "Oh Angus what can you be thinking of?" screams my mother rushing protectively toward me.

"Mary, please!" says my father almost desperately, "there's nothing wrong."

My grandfather gets up very rapidly, sets me on the chair he has just vacated, drains the controversial glass, rinses it in the sink and says, "Well, time for the working class to be in bed. Good-night all." He goes up the stairs walking very heavily and we can hear his boots as he thumps them on the floor.

17

"I'll put him to bed, Mary," says my father nodding toward me. "I know where he sleeps. Why don't you go to bed now? You're tired."

"Yes, all right," says my mother very gently. "I'm sorry. I didn't mean to hurt his feelings. Good-night." She kisses me and also my grandmother and her footsteps fade quietly up the stairs.

"I'm sorry Ma, she didn't mean it the way it sounded," says my father.

"I know. She finds it very different from what she's used to. And we are older and don't bounce back the way we once did. He is seventy-six now and the mine is hard on him and he feels he must work harder than ever to do his share. He works with different ones of the boys and he tells me that sometimes he thinks they are carrying him just because he is their father. He never felt that way with you or Alex but of course you were all much younger then. Still he always somehow felt that because those years between high school and college were so good that you would both come back to him some day."

"But Ma, it can't be that way. I was twenty then and Alex nineteen and he was only in his early fifties and we both wanted to go to college so we could be something else. And we paid him back the money he loaned us and he seemed to want us to go to school then."

"He did not know what it was then. Nor I. And when you gave him back the money it was as if that was not what he'd had in mind at all. And what is the something you two became? A lawyer whom we never see and a doctor who committed suicide when he was twenty-seven. Lost to us the both of you. More lost than Andrew who is buried under tons of rock two miles beneath the sea and who never saw a college door."

"Well, he should have," says my father bitterly, "so should they all instead of being exploited and burrowing beneath the sea or becoming alcoholics that cannot even do that."

"I have my alcoholic," says my grandmother now standing very tall, "who was turned out of my Montreal lawyer's home."

18

"But I couldn't do anything with him, Ma, and it's different there. You just can't be that way, and — and — oh hell, I don't know; if I were by myself he could have stayed forever."

"I know," says my grandmother now very softly, putting her hand upon his shoulder, "it's not you. But it seems that we can only stay forever if we stay right here. As we have stayed to the seventh generation. Because in the end that is all there is — just staying. I have lost three children at birth but I've raised eight sons. I have one a lawyer and one a doctor who committed suicide, one who died in coal beneath the sea and one who is a drunkard and four who still work the coal like their father and those four are all that I have that stand by me. It is these four that carry their father now that he needs it, and it is these four that carry the drunkard, that dug two days for Andrew's body and that have given me thirty grandchildren in my old age."

"I know, Ma," says my father, "I know that and I appreciate it all, everything. It is just that, well somehow we just can't live in a clan system anymore. We have to see beyond ourselves and our own families. We have to live in the twentieth century."

"Twentieth century?" says my grandmother spreading her big hands across her checkered apron. "What is the twentieth century to me if I cannot have my own?"

It is morning now and I awake to the argument of the English sparrows outside my window and the fingers of the sun upon the floor. My parents are in my room discussing my clothes. "He really doesn't need them," says my father patiently. "But Angus I don't want him to look like a little savage," replies my mother as she lays out my newly pressed pants and shirt at the foot of the bed.

Downstairs I learn that my grandfather has already gone to work and as I solemnly eat my breakfast like a little old man beyond my years, I listen to the violin music on the radio and watch my grandmother as she spreads butter on the top of the baking loaves and pokes the coals of her fire with a fierce enthusiasm that sends clouds of smoke billowing up to spread themselves against the yellowed paint upon her ceiling.

Then the little boys come in and stand shyly against the wall. There are seven of them and they are all between six and ten. "These are your cousins," says my grandmother to me and to them she says, "this is Alex from Montreal. He is come to visit with us and you are to be nice to him because he is one of our own."

Then I and my cousins go outside because it is what we are supposed to do and we ask one another what grades we are in and I say I dislike my teacher and they mostly say they like theirs which is a possibility I have never considered before. And then we talk about hockey and I try to remember the times I have been to the Forum in Montreal and what I think about Richard.

And then we go down through the town which is black and smoky and has no nice streets nor flashing lights like Montreal, and when I dawdle behind I suddenly find myself confronted by two older boys who say: "Hey, where'd'y get them sissy clothes?" I do not know what I am supposed to do until my cousins come back and surround me like the covered wagons around the women and children of the cowboy shows, when the Indians attack.

"This is our cousin," say the oldest two simultaneously and I think they are very fine and brave for they too are probably a little bit ashamed of me and I wonder if I would do the same for them. I have never before thought that perhaps I have been lonely all of my short life and I wish that I had brothers of my own — even sisters perhaps.

My almost-attackers wait a while scuffing their shoes on the ashy sidewalk and then they separate and allow us to pass like a little band of cavalry going through the mountains.

We continue down through the town and farther beyond to the seashore where the fishermen are mending their gear and pumping the little boats in which they allow us to play. Then we skip rocks on the surface of the sea and I skip one six times and then stop because I know I have made an impression and doubt if I am capable of an encore.

And then we climb up a high, high hill that tumbles into the sea and a cousin says we will go to see the bull who apparently lives about a mile away. We are really out in the country now and it is getting hot and when I go to loosen my tie the collar button comes off and is forever lost in the grass through which we pass.

The bull lives in a big barn and my cousins ask an old man who looks like my grandfather if he expects any cows today. He says that he does not know, that you cannot tell about those things. We can look at the bull if we wish but we must not tease him nor go too close. He is very big and brown and white with a ring in his nose and he paws the floor of his stall and makes low noises while lowering his head and swinging it from side to side. Just as we are ready to leave the old man comes in carrying a long wooden staff which he snaps onto the bull's nose ring. "Well, it looks like you laddies are in luck," he says, "now be careful and get out of the way." I follow my cousins who run out into a yard where a man who has just arrived is standing holding a nervous cow by a halter and we sit appreciatively on the top rail of the wooden fence and watch the old man as he leads out the bull who is now moaning and dripping and frothing at the mouth. I have never seen anything like this before and watch with awe this something that is both beautiful and terrible and I know that I will somehow not be able to tell my mother to whom I have told almost everything important that has happened in my young life.

And later as we leave, the old man's wife gives us some apples and says, "John you should be ashamed of yourself; in front of these children. There are some things that have to be but are not for children's eyes." The chastised old man nods and looks down upon his shoes but then looks up at us very gravely from beneath his bushy eyebrows, looks at us in a very special way and I know that it is only because we are all boys that he does this and that the look as it excludes the woman simultaneously includes us in something that I know and feel but cannot understand.

21

We go back then to the town and it is late afternoon and we have eaten nothing but the apples and as we climb the hill toward my grandparents' house I see my father striding down upon us with his newspaper under his arm.

He is not disturbed that I have stayed away so long and seems almost to envy us our unity and our dirt as he stands so straight and lonely in the prison of his suit and inquires of our day. And so we reply as children do, that we have been "playing," which is the old inadequate message sent forth across the chasm of our intervening years to fall undelivered and unreceived into the nothingness between.

He is going down to the mine, he says, to meet the men when they come off their shift at four and he will take me if I wish. So I separate from my comrade-cousins and go back down the hill holding on to his hand which is something I do not often do. I think that I will tell him about the bull but instead I ask: "Why do all the men chew tobacco?"

"Oh," he says, "because it is a part of them and of their way of life. They do that instead of smoking."

"But why don't they smoke?"

"Because they are underground so much of their lives and they cannot light a match or a lighter or carry any open flame down there. It's because of the gas. Flame might cause an explosion and kill them all."

"But, when they're not down there they could smoke cigarettes like Grandpa Gilbert in a silver cigarette holder and Mama says that chewing tobacco is a filthy habit."

"I know but these people are not all like Grandpa Gilbert and there are things that Mama doesn't understand. It is not that easy to change what is a part of you."

We are approaching the mine now and everything is black and grimy and the heavily laden trucks are groaning past us. "Did you used to chew tobacco?"

"Yes, a very long time ago before you were ever thought of."

"And was it hard for you to stop?"

22

"Yes it was, Alex," he says quietly, "more difficult than you will ever know."

We are now at the wash-house and the trains from the underground are thundering up out of the darkness and the men are jumping off and laughing and shouting to one another in a way that reminds me of recess. They are completely black with the exception of little white half-moons beneath their eyes and the eyes themselves. My grandfather is walking toward us between two of my uncles. He is not so tall as they nor does he take such long strides and they are pacing themselves to keep even with him the way my father sometimes does with me. Even his moustache is black or a very dirty grey except for the bottom of it where the tobacco stains it brown.

As they walk they are taking off their headlamps and unfastening the batteries from the broad belts which I feel would be very fine for carrying holsters and six-guns. They are also fishing for the little brass discs which bear their identification numbers. My father says that if they should be killed in the underground these little discs would tell who each man was. It does not seem like much consolation to me.

At a wicket that looks like the post office the men line up and pass their lamps and the little discs to an old man with glasses. He puts the lamps on a rack and the disks on a large board behind his back. Each disc goes on its special little numbered hook and this shows that its owner has returned. My grandfather is 572.

Inside the adjoining wash-house it is very hot and steamy like when you are in a bathroom a long, long time with the hot water running. There are long rows of numbered lockers with wooden benches before them. The floor is cement with little wooden slatted paths for the men to walk on as they pass barefooted to and from the noisy showers at the building's farthest end.

"And did you have a good day today Alex?" asks my grandfather as we stop before his locker. And then unexpectedly and before I can reply he places his two big hands on either side of my head and turns it back and forth very powerfully upon my shoulders. I can feel the pressure of his calloused fingers squeezing hard against my cheeks and pressing my ears into my head and I can feel the fine, fine, coal dust which I know is covering my face and I can taste it from his thumbs which are close against my lips. It is not gritty as I had expected but is more like smoke than sand and almost like my mother's powder. And now he presses my face into his waist and holds me there for a long, long time with my nose bent over against the blackened buckle of his belt. Unable to see or hear or feel or taste or smell anything that is not black; holding me there engulfed and drowning in blackness until I am unable to breathe.

And my father is saying from a great distance: "What are you doing? Let him go! He'll suffocate." And then the big hands come away from my ears and my father's voice is louder and he sounds like my mother.

Now I am so black that I am almost afraid to move and the two men are standing over me looking into one another's eyes. "Oh, well," says my grandfather turning reluctantly toward his locker and beginning to open his shirt.

"I guess there is only one thing to do now," says my father quietly and he bends down slowly and pulls loose the laces of my shoes. Soon I am standing naked upon the wooden slats and my grandfather is the same beside me and then he guides and follows me along the wooden path that leads us to the showers and away from where my father sits. I look back once and see him sitting all alone on the bench which he has covered with his newspaper so that his suit will not be soiled.

When I come to the door of the vast shower room I hesitate because for a moment I feel afraid but I feel my grandfather strong and hairy behind me and we venture out into the pouring water and the lathered, shouting bodies and the cakes of skidding yellow soap. We cannot find a shower at first until one of my uncles shouts to us and a soap-covered man points us in the right direction. We are already wet and the blackness of my grandfather's face is running down in two grey rivulets from the corners of his moustache.

My uncle at first steps out of the main stream but then the three of us stand and move and wash beneath the torrent that spills upon us. The soap is very yellow and strong. It smells like the men's washroom in Montreal Forum and my grandfather tells me not to get it in my eyes. Before we leave he gradually turns off the hot water and increases the cold. He says this is so we will not catch cold when we leave. It gets colder and colder but he tells me to stay under it as long as I can and I am covered with goose pimples and my teeth are chattering when I jump out for the last time. We walk back through the washing men who are not so numerous now. Then along the wooden path and I look at the tracks our bare feet leave behind.

My father is still sitting on the bench by himself as we had left him. He is glad to see us return, and smiles. My grandfather takes two heavy towels out of his locker and after we are dry he puts on his clean clothes and I put on the only ones I have except the bedraggled tie which my father stuffs into his pocket. So we go out into the sun and walk up the long, long hill and I am allowed to carry the lunch pail with the thermos bottle rattling inside. We walk very slowly and say very little. Every once in a while my grandfather stops and turns to look back the way we have come. It is very beautiful. The sun is moving into the sea as if it is tired and the sea is very blue and very wide — wide enough it seems for a hundred suns. It touches the sand of the beach which is a slender boundary of gold separating the blue from the greenness of the grass which comes rolling down upon it. Then there is the mine silhouetted against it all, looking like a toy from a meccano set; yet its bells ring as the coal-laden cars fly up out of the deep, grumble as they are unloaded, and flee with thundering power down the slopes they leave behind. Then the blackened houses begin and march row and row up the hill to where we stand and beyond to where we go. Overhead the gulls are flying inland, slowly but steadily as if they are somehow very sure of everything. My grandfather says they always fly inland in the evening. They have done so as long as he can remember.

And now we are entering the yard and my mother is rushing toward me and pressing me to her and saying to everyone and no one, "Where has this child been all day? I have been almost out of my mind." She buries her fingers in my hair and I feel very sorry for my mother because I think she loves me very much. "Playing," I say.

At supper I am so tired that I can hardly sit up at the table and my father takes me to bed before it is yet completely dark. I wake up once when I hear my parents talking softly at the door. "I am trying very hard. I really am," says my mother. "Yes, yes I know you are," says my father gently and they move off down the hall.

And now it is in the morning two weeks later and the train that takes us back will be leaving very soon. All our suitcases are in the taxi and the good-byes are almost all completed. I am the last to leave my grandmother as she stands beside her stove. She lifts me up as she did the first night and says, "Good-bye Alex, you are the only grandchild I will never know," and presses into my hand the crinkled dollar that is never spent.

My grandfather is not in although he has not gone to work and they say he has walked on ahead of us to the station. We bump down the hill to where the train is waiting beside the small brown building and he is on the platform talking with some other men and spitting tobacco over the side.

He walks over to us and everyone says good-bye at once. I am again the last and he shakes hands very formally this time. "Good-bye Alex," he says, "it was ten years before you saw me. In another ten I will not be here to see." And then I get on the train and none too soon for already it is beginning to move. Everyone waves but the train goes on because it must and it does not care for waving. From very far away I see my grandfather turn and begin walking back up his hill. And then there is nothing but the creak and sway of the coach and the blue sea with its gulls and the green hills with the gashes of their coal imbedded deeply in their sides. And we do not say anything but sit silent and alone. We have come from a great distance and have a long way now to go.

The red wool shirt

Alden Nowlan

I was hanging out my wash,
says the woman in North Sydney.
It was a rope line I was using
and they were wooden pins,
the real old-fashioned kind
that didn't have a spring.

It was good drying weather.

I could see the weir fishermen
at work.
    I had a red wool shirt
in my hands and had just
noticed that one of the buttons
was missing.

Then I looked up and saw
Charlie Sullivan coming
towards me.
He'd always had a funny walk.
It was as if he was walking
sideways.
    That walk of his
always made me smile except
for some reason
I didn't smile
that day.
    He had on a hat
with salmon flies
that he'd tied himself
in the brim.

Poor old Charlie.

It's bad, Mary, he said.

I finished
hanging up the red wool
shirt
        and then I said,
Charlie, it's not
both of them, and he said,
Mary, I'm afraid it is.

And that was that.

from Each Man's Son

Hugh MacLennan

At the top of the cliff they paused, breathless, and looked back over the sea. Its blue was deeper than the blue of the sky and the black hull and white sails of the schooner were tiny on its surface. Waves three miles long swelled in from far out and burst in lines of slow, lazy foam down the length of the coast. The woman and the boy stood watching until the distance made their eyes ache and then they turned inland. A few sheep, their shadows spindlelegged on the common where they pastured at the cliff's edge, looked up and baaed at them. They walked over the treeless pasture, climbed a stile and descended on the other side to a rough path which led them homeward through a low growth of brush and brambles.

Before them to the right stood the colliery. Black and monstrous it bulged against the western sky, a huge mountain of coal with the bankhead seemingly on top of it, a trestle beside the coal bank supporting a square-boilered locomotive with a short rain of cradle cars behind it. From this distance the train looked like a column of black ants that had crawled up the stalk of a gigantic plant and died there.

This was the visible colliery. Without framing their thoughts, both Mollie MacNeil and her son knew that what they saw behind the wire fence was merely the product of the last two weeks of work. A hundred fathoms beneath the ground they were walking on ran the seam. Galleries like the tentacles of an octopus branched out beneath the floor of the sea itself, and it was in these galleries that the men of the families in their neighborhood went down each day and came up again. They also knew that theirs was only one of some fifteen collieries which circled the town of Broughton. They felt lucky because theirs was so close to the sea.

Mollie and her son skirted the colliery fence, its enclosed area quiet as a church since the men had quit work, and finally they reached the main road which came from Broughton and then, after passing the colliery fence, made a right-angled turn and ran down a steep slope to a bridge over a bubbling brook. Between the bridge and the colliery, for a distance of two hundred and fifty yards, crowded so close together they looked like a single downward-slanting building with a single downward-slanting roof, were the houses of the miner's row.

Mollie looked at Alan and smiled. "There now," she said. "We're almost home."

Somewhere in the row was a door which they called their own, but nothing distinguished it from the doors to right or left of it. Each house was a square with a triangle set on its top. There were two doors side by side in the front of each one and on either side of the doors were single windows behind which lurked small parlors. The houses were divided in two by a common wall between the doors, behind each parlor at the back of the buildings was a kitchen, and upstairs under sharply sloping roofs, were the bedrooms. The houses had all been painted the same fierce shade of iron oxide red when they were built by the coal company; two families shared each sloping roof; all of them used a rickety board sidewalk which ran between the low doorsteps and the road. Between the sidewalk and the road was a deep ditch overgrown with thistle, burdock and coarse grass, and down the center of the road, making a right-angled turn at the corner by the colliery, ran the tracks of the tramline which bound the collieries to their heart in Broughton.

Tonight as Mollie and Alan passed the tram stop and went their way down the board sidewalk there was activity along the whole row. Before each house, beside each low doorstep, a washtub had been set on a stool. In front of each tub a miner just back from the pit crouched, stripped to the waist, while his wife, working hard with both arms, scrubbed the coal dust off his face, neck, back, shoulders and arms. Mollie and Alan passed them one by one and Mollie exchanged greetings with some of the wives. There was a loud splashing of water and a grunting and spitting from the men as the two figures went by, but the boy saw no adventure in the scene. It had been this same way every night of his life when the weather was warm.

In the kitchen that evening, after they finished their supper, Alan took the sea shell from his pocket and held it against his ear.

"Mummy, listen!"

He handed her the shell and she also held it against her ear. "All shells sound like that," she said. "They remember the sea."

"How can they remember? They're not alive."

Her face lightened as she thought of an answer. "It was in the book we read with the birds and snakes and fish. It said that the first things that ever lived were in the sea. Are you listening, Alan? That means the shell is so old the noise in it is the oldest sound in the world."

She was pleased because he seemed to be satisfied and for a moment she watched him as he listened to the shell. Then she looked at the alarm clock on the shelf over the table and told him it was late and past his bedtime. He got up and went upstairs slowly, knowing that because it was Saturday night his mother would be going out. Under the sharp slant of the roof he took off his shirt and hung it on a nail. Then he took off his pants and finally his shoes and stockings. He laid his shoes side by side on the floor by the head of his cot and carefully pressed down the creases in his pants before he laid them on a wooden chair. He turned the socks inside out and laid them on the back of the chair and finally took a flannelette nightgown from under his pillow and put it on. The shell went under the pillow where the nightgown had been, he scrambled into bed and pulled the covers up to his chin and lay on his back.

"Mummy," he called. "I'm here."

A moment later he heard the stairs creak and then she came in and looked quickly to see how well he had disposed of his clothes.

"Now," she said, and smiled at him as she sat on the edge of his cot. "You're all ready for sleep."

"No. I'm not sleepy."

"But that is the time you grow, and think how strong you must grow if your father is going to be pleased when he comes home."

Alan's voice was muffled. "Does Father remember me?"

"Of course he does."

"Donald's father doesn't have to remember him. He comes home every night."

She slipped off the edge of the cot and sat down on the floor beside him, to make her serious face on a level with his. "Look at me, Alan."

He turned on his side to face her.

"Now, don't ever, ever forget. You have one of the most special fathers of anybody you've ever heard of. He is not like Donald's father, coming home every night with the pit dust all over his face so you can't tell who he is."

The boy began to smile.

"Archie MacNeil," she said the name proudly. "It is something to be the son of the bravest man in Cape Breton." She stood up and looked down at him. "But you must do your part and grow strong so he will be pleased when he comes home. It is hard for a boy not to have his father with him every night. It is

33

hard for me, too. But think how much he misses us. Your father is so special that he had to go out into the world to do his work."

She went back into the parlor and took off her hat. She looked at the rug and even picked up the hook, then she laid it down again. She touched a match to the wick in the lamp, turned it low, and then stood for some minutes considering her reflection in the mirror. She did not think she had changed much. Archie would find little difference in her if he came home now. An idea crossed her mind and she looked about the room until her eyes found a small framed photograph on the top shelf of the whatnot. She took it down and went back to the mirror, comparing her reflection with the girl in the picture until she admitted to herself that she had changed a great deal. She looked no more than a child in that wedding photograph as she stood hanging onto Archie's arm. They had both been so young; Archie twenty and she three years younger. She looked at Archie's thick hair and remembered the way it felt when her fingers brushed it the wrong way. He had never been able to part his hair, it had been so stiff. Even in that poor picture his eyes looked hurt and exposed, and no wonder, she thought, with the life his father had made for him. She had been the first person in all Broughton to understand and admire Archie — before he became a hero whom nobody understood and everyone admired.

She put the photograph back on the whatnot and then sighed without realizing she was doing so, as she passed the palms of her hands down the neat curves of her hips and flanks. For the first time in four years a thought opened wide in her mind as she tried to examine it. Would Archie ever come home? It was more than a year since he had sent any money and eight months since she had even received a postcard from him. But she knew where he was at the moment, and that was a lot more than she usually knew about him.

Did Archie ever intend to come home? She put the thought away again as she pulled open a drawer in the table by the window and took out a piece of newspaper which she had folded and stuffed in there the day before. Spreading it out flat on the table, she turned up the lamp and began to read it slowly, beginning with the Halifax dateline under the banner on the sports page. Archie's name was often to be found in this column, but never before had there been so much.

Up from New York comes word that Archie MacNeil's next opponent is being groomed for a shot at Jack Dillon's light-heavyweight title. They say this boy Packy Miller is quite a slugger and you can get odds at four to one that he'll beat Archie, and two to one he'll win by the knockout route. The fight's to be held in Trenton, New Jersey, by the way, Miller's home town.

If these odds are anywhere near right, all we can say is that Archie has gone a long way over the hill. We saw Packy Miller in Boston last fall, and the boy who fought that night couldn't have stayed in the same ring with the Archie MacNeil who flattened Tim O'Leary two years ago that great night in Providence.

Mollie remembered the fight with O'Leary, remembered what Archie's victory had meant to the men of Broughton and all the collieries roundabout. They had been as happy as though something beautiful had come into the lives of them all. She read on.

Archie's decline from the status of top-line contender to a trail horse fighting for peanuts calls for some pretty sharp questions about how well he's been managed. A long time ago — three months after the O'Leary fight to be exact — this column noted that Archie MacNeil was battling at the rate of once every ten days. What fighter can stand a pace like that? He was sent in at catchweights against George Chip before his left eye was healed from an

35

old cut. Chip was ten pounds lighter, but he also happened to be the middleweight champion of the world, and what he did to Archie's eye that night wasn't funny. To our way of thinking, that particular fight was the turning point in the career of the boy from the mines.

Make no mistake, this boy Packy Miller is no George Chip. The odds may be heavy, but we have a hunch that Archie is going to win this one. He better had, because if he can't beat Miller there's no place else for him to go.

Mollie read that last sentence over again and tried to realize that the words referred to her husband. When she and Archie were married there had been no question of his becoming a prize fighter. That he was a brave and a good boxer she had known; so were lots of other guys in Broughton. She had known that he was fierce, unpredictable, hated his work in the mine and some-times got roaring drunk. So did many others. But she had always been able to quiet him and control him until he was calm again. Alan was too little to remember the excitement when his father won the middleweight championship of Canada in a fight in Halifax, thereby astonishing and delighting the whole of Cape Breton Island. Then the fat man with the bowler hat had come up from the Boston States to offer him big money for fighting.

Mollie closed her eyes and clasped her hands as she remem-bered the man. He had been so dreadful and Archie had not been able to see it. He was fat and pasty and his voice was a thin falsetto. He had only half a nose, and when she asked Archie what had happened to it, Archie laughed and told her somebody had bitten it off years ago. That was the first time she had felt a whisper of fear that she might lose Archie. His lovely body — wide in the shoulders, narrow in the waist with rippling muscles all over — this was to be turned into a punching machine by an ugly fat man whose name was Sam Downey.

But to the men of Broughton, Archie was a hero. When he gave an exhibition before going away, six thousand Highlanders

— men who had been driven from the outdoors into the pits where physical courage had become almost the only virtue they could see clearly and see all the time — paid to watch him fight. They loved him because he was giving significance, even a crude beauty, to the clumsy courage they all felt in themselves.

The Springhill Mining Disaster

Ewan MacColl
Peggy Seeger

One of the most tragic, most heroic and most poignant events in
recent Canadian history was the mine cave-in at Springhill,
Nova Scotia in the fall of 1958. What made it noteworthy
was not only the sadness for those who died, or the tales of
bravery by those who survived, but the fact that it meant —
practically — the death of a town and a way of life.

In the town of Springhill, Nova Scotia,
Down in the dark of the Cumberland Mine,
There's blood on the coal and the miners lie,
In roads that never saw sun nor sky,
Roads that never saw sun nor sky.

In the town of Springhill you don't sleep easy,
Often the earth will tremble and roll,
When the earth is restless, miners die,
Bone and blood is the price of coal.

In the town of Springhill, Nova Scotia,
Late in the year of fifty-eight,
Day still comes and the sun still shines,
But it's dark as a grave in the Cumberland Mine.

Down at the coal face miners working
Rattle of the belts and the cutter's blade,
Crumble of rock and the walls close around,
Living and the dead men two miles down.

Twelve men lay two miles from the pit-shaft,
Twelve men lay in the dark and sang,
Long hot days in a miner's tomb,
Three feet high and a hundred long.

Three days passed and the lamps gave out,

And Kaleb Rushton he up and said,
"There's no more water nor light nor bread,
So we'll live on songs and hope instead."

Listen for the shouts of the bare-faced miners,
Listen through the rubble for a rescue team,
Six hundred feet of coal and slag,
Hope imprisoned in a three-foot seam.

Eight days passed and some were rescued,
Leaving the dead to lie alone,
Through all their lives they dug their grave,
Two miles of earth for a marking stone.

In the town of Springhill, Nova Scotia,
Down in the dark of the Cumberland Mine,
There's blood on the coal and the miners lie,
In roads that never saw sun nor sky,
Roads that never saw sun nor sky.

The Land

The land under this house
is weak, girl

you can't tell by looking
at it
but, see
its all mined out
under here
and we're after sittin on
a bridge over caves

Now the other week
old Cameron down the road
dropped clean out of sight
into a hole

Drivin along now
mind, not out to harm a fly
dropped twenty foot
down
clean out of sight

Had to bring MacNeil
the fire chief
down in town
to come haul'em out

But nobody was surprised, eh?

Look, years ago
Dominion Coal
dried up these here wells
mining all under the town
minin

ya. and there we were with no water

What did they do?

Well I'll tell you what they did
brought a little truck around
every day

and every family
got two buckets of water
whether they needed it
or not.
Ha.
There's no support'all girl

Hell, no one was surprised
when old Cameron and his heap
went straight down

the company took it all,
see
whether they needed it or not.
Ha.

The Nova Scotian owns his own name
and answers to it without hesitation at the challenge
of whatever roll call. He owns his own blood.
And his is the most remembering of all bloods.
The tincture of heritage from that of his forbears
is always constitutively in him in the miraculous way
that a single tear is said to tincture, with its
disinfectant, seas of water; in the way that a man's
resemblance to his great-grandparent across the forehead
is transmitted in a pinpoint of sperm.
Even now, the gait of original freedom stubbornly
in him and his fellows, he never has to go far
to find another Nova Scotian with a like spine:
to match itself against annihilation by the
juggernaut which levels all things to sameness.
Enough of these men may yet stop it dead in its tracks.
Their spirit may yet prevail, as the simplest green plant
can split the clench of stone
and break out its green leaves above it.

Aye! no monuments

Rita Joe

Ai! Mu knu'kaqann,
Mu nuji-wi'kikaqann,
Mu weskitaqawikasinukl kisna
   mikekni-napuikasinukl
Kekinua'tuenukl wlakue'l
   pa'qalaiwaqann.

Ta'n teluji-mtua'lukwi'tij nuji-
kina'mua'tijik a.

Ke'kwilmi'tij,
Maqamikewe'l wisunn,
Apaqte'l wisunn,
Sipu'l;
Mukk kasa'tu mikuite'tmaqanmk
Wula knu'kaqann.

Ki' kelu'lk nemitmikl
Kmtne'l samqwann nisitk,
Kesikawitkl sipu'l.
Wula na kis-napui'kmu'kl
Mikuite'tmaqanminaq.
Nuji-kina'masultioq,
   we'jitutoqsip ta'n kisite'mekl

Wisunn aqq ta'n pa'qi-klu'lk,
Tepqatmi'tij Lnu weja'tekemk
   weji-nsituita'timk.

Aye! no monuments,
No literature,
No scrolls or canvas-drawn pictures
Relate the wonders of our yesterday.

How frustrated the searchings
   of the educators.

Let them find
Land names,
Titles of seas,
Rivers;
Wipe them not from memory.
These are our monuments.

Breathtaking views-
Waterfalls on a mountain,
Fast flowing rivers.
These are our sketches
Committed to our memory.
Scholars, you will find our art
In names and scenery,
Betrothed to the Indian
   since time began.

from The Clockmaker

Thomas Chandler Haliburton

I had heard of Yankee clock-pedlars, tin-pedlars, and bible-ped-
lars, especially of him who sold Polyglot Bibles (all in *English*) to
the amount of sixteen thousand pounds. The house of every substantial farmer had three substantial ornaments: a wooden
clock, a tin reflector, and a Polyglot Bible. How is it that an
American can sell his wares at whatever price he pleases, where
a Bluenose would fail to make a sale at all? I will enquire of the
Clockmaker the secret of his success.

"What a pity it is Mr. Slick" (for such was his name), "what
a pity it is," said I, "that you, who are so successful in teaching
these people the value of clocks, could not also teach them the
value of time."

"I guess," said he, "they have got that ring to grow on their
horns yet, which every four-year-old has in our country. We
reckon hours and minutes to be dollars and cents. They do nothin' in these parts but eat, drink, smoke, sleep, ride about, lounge
at taverns, make speeches at temperance meetin's, and talk
about 'House of Assembly.' If a man don't hoe his corn and
don't get a crop, he says it is all owin' to the bank; and if he runs
into debt and is sued, why, he says the lawyers are a curse to the
country. They are a most idle set of folks, I tell you."

from The Clockmaker's Opinion of Halifax

"You appear," said I, "to have travelled over the whole of this province and to have observed the country and the people with much attention. Pray what is your opinion of the present state and future prospects of Halifax?"

"If you will tell me," said he, "when the folks there will wake up, then I can answer you; but they're fast asleep. As to the province, it's a splendid province, and calkilated to go ahead. It will grow as fast as a Varginny gal; and they grow so amazin' fast, if you put your arm round one of their necks to kiss 'em, by the time you've done, they've grow'd up into women. It's a pretty province, I tell you, good above and better below; surface covered with pastur's, meadows, woods and a 'nation sight of water privileges, and onder the ground full of mines:

.   .   .

"Now, this province is ... good enough at top, but dip down and you have the riches: the coal, the iron ore, the gypsum, and what not. As for Halifax, it's well enough in itself, though no great shakes neither — a few sizable houses, with a proper sight of small ones, like half a dozen old hens with their broods of young chickens; but the people, the strange critters, they're all asleep. ...

"Halifax reminds me of a Russian officer I once see'd at

46

Warsaw; he had lost both arms in battle . . .; [he was] a good natur'd, contented critter as I e'en a'most ever see'd, and he was fed with spoons by his neighbours; but a'ter a while they grew tired of it, and I guess he near about starved to death at last. Now Halifax is like that 'are 'spooney,' as I used to call him; it is fed by the outports, and they begin to have enough to do to feed themselves: it must larn to live without 'em. They have no river and no country about them; let 'em make a railroad to Minas Basin, and they will have arms of their own to feed themselves with. If they don't do it, and do it soon, I guess they'll get into a decline that no human skill will cure. They are proper thin now; you can count their ribs e'en a'most as far as you can see them. The *only* thing that will either make or save Halifax is a railroad across the country to Bay of Fundy.

"   'It will do to talk of,' says one. 'You'll see it some day," says another. 'Yes,' says a third, 'it will come, but we are too young yet. . . . ' In the meantime, the young folks wun't wait and run off to the States, where the maxim is: 'Youth is the time for improvement; a new country is never too young for exertion: push on, keep movin', *go ahead.*'

"Darn it all!" said the Clockmaker, rising with great animation, clenching his fist, and extending his arm. "Darn it all; it fairly makes my dander rise to see the nasty, idle, loungin', good-for-nothing, do-little critters; they ain't fit to tend a bear-trap, I vow. They ought to be quilted round and round a room, like a lady's lap-dog, the matter of two hours a day, to keep 'em from dyin' of apoplexy. . . . "

Old N.S.

Fraser Sutherland

Here people stay the same. They don't bend,
alter, shift, or move perceptibly.
They're somewhere in behind the landscape,
hiding back of trees. They only come out
when the white light of Progress beams
upon them. Then they're etched sharply.
Sometimes they're seen
flitting from blackened stump to stump,
seeking cover. They become what people
tell them, yet stay stubbornly
the same. Moving away, you're a strange
native son, remaining, stranger still.
The softness comes after the salt,
highways meld with logging trails;
you meet folks, are yourself embarrassed,
slightly flustered at your knowledge of them, of
yourself. This is one sea-road. The rest
is stark raving reality.

Girls In The Parlor

Charles Bruce

THEY have held funerals and weddings here.
And on the wall, in cardboard and dull gilt,
They keep the faces, bearded, stern, austere,
Of men who cleared the place, and plowed and built   —

And women: bold, shy, laughing, sensitive,
Or stiff with pride, in frills of lace and lawn,
Who came serenely to this house to live
And brought their girlhood with them, and are gone.

This is the room they held against the claims
Of earth and sea and time — the touch of grace.
And you can see them in their oval frames
In gowns of buttoned satin, and white lace.

Seventeen Forty-Nine

Bill Howell

Who cares who we've been? Those without roots
will never forgive those of us with them.   ...

Weren't we the first Free Enterprisers here,
the ones who first helped haul the bells up
into old St. Paul's? Merchants from Bristol,
Portsmouth, and Liverpool, who came back
to the Banks with Cabot, and stayed
where "the fish slowed the progress
of our ships." The guys who laughed
at Humphrey Gilbert's plumes at St. John's
harbour, who made *money* while Hudson and Frobisher
were busy busting their asses for us. The guys
who were pressed into the Royal Navy, who turned
back the Armada. The guys who finally had enough
of England when England gave Louisbourg back, but
who went on anyway, because we've never run
from a fight we couldn't win, to take Quebec,
the Great Rock, the Key to All.   ... Pity
the poor WASP, who has to sting himself first.   ...

For don't we all make up our own histories
as we go, those of us who are "doing well"?

My father, bred and buttered in Portsmouth,
took me and my brother across the Great Sea
to this New World at ten months of age
from Abercrombie Hospital in Liverpool, and
we giggled and bawled the whole way over.
If that isn't formative, what is? My mother,
a Loyalist from St. John, lost her grandmother's
brooch playing Madame La Tour in high school,
and still loves to holiday in New England,
searching for distant, lost, Yankee relations.

And we all have cousins who hid the Expulsion out
in the Gaspereaux Hills. And cousins who gave
diesel oil to Nazi u-boats outside Lunenburg
just before I was born. ... Pity the poor WASP,
who has to sting himself last. ...
But how long have we been sleeping here,
beside our secret memory, the sea?

Too soon we seem old inside our trusty dream. ...
("Ah yes, bye, and we'd do it all again, by God!")
Most important of the things that don't work
in this city are the guns on Citadel Hill. ...
("And ah, she's a fine side, that one!")
And the noonday gun is just a vain attempt
to kill the rest of the afternoon. ...
("And there's always some pretty lively
steppers in the distance. ...")
There's a Zumburger stand in Scotia Square,
and nobody knows what *that* means. ...
("And you can always tell a man from his hands.")
And all the old electric Beltline trolley buses,
outdated with so many other dates around,
have been sold for a *fine* price to Toronto. ...
("And inland, bye, the continent starts from *here*!")
And here, bellbottoms will always be fashionable. ...

So shall we sell them Tidal Power
or tell them seabirds rule the world?

The Amazing Cannon at Liverpool, N.S.

Joseph Sherman

Liverpool has the greatest cannon in the world
    aged firm resolute
their backs fitting snugly
    between a small boy's knees
    bare legs rubbing each mottled flank
with terrible ridged mouths
    set to rattle navies

I recall two
    facing against the thin steady waves
and me crouched low along a black spine
    eyes following the angle of the snout
    out over the heads of all others
    walking along distantly
    over the frail pebbles

From my very first lookout till my last
    I searched for sail
    till my eyes gave in
then for a radio mast
    and finally in desperation
    for the bare flick of an oar
    sneaking through the fog
anything on which to unleash my power

Winter's Tale

Thomas Raddall

The air in the classroom was warm and rather stuffy because it had snowed a little the night before, and Stevens the janitor had stoked up his great furnace fiercely. Grade Nine, coming in rosy-cheeked from the snow outside, found it oppressive, but nobody dared to open a window. Old Mr. Burtle, who conducted the educational fortunes of Grade Nine, was Principal of the school and a martyr to asthma.

The rest of the big brick school was empty and silent. The lower grades were not required to answer roll-call until half-past nine. It was just one minute past nine by the clock on the class-room wall when James hung his school-bag on the back of his seat and flung an arithmetic manual on the desk. He also produced two pencils and sharpened them with his jack-knife, dropping the shavings on the floor and keeping a wary eye on Old Gander Burtle, who disapproved of that procedure. All about him was a bustle of preparation. Fifty boys and girls were busy with books, pencils, and erasers.

"Attention!" demanded Old Gander, with his asthmatic cough. Everybody sat up very straight. "We shall sing the morning hymn." The class arose with a clatter, shuffled a little, and then burst raucously into "Awake my soul and with the sun" as Old Gander raised his bony forefinger. James had a point of vantage when they stood up to sing; for his desk was near the windows and he could look down into the street, two storeys below. It was certainly too nice a morning to spend indoors. The sky was blue, without a speck of cloud anywhere, sun very bright on the snow, and wisps of smoke rising straight into the air from a forest of chimneys that stretched away southward. The snow was not deep enough for sleighing. There were a few wheel-tracks in the street, and the sidewalks were a mess of brown slush already, and when the several hundred kids of the lower grades had scampered in, there would be nothing but thin black puddles. Grade Nine intoned a long "Ahhh-men!" and sat down. It was five minutes past nine by the clock on the wall.

The act of sitting down in unison always produced a clatter, but this morning the effect was astounding. The hardwood floor began to move up and down very rapidly, like a gigantic piston of some sort; the walls swayed drunkenly to and fro, so that the blackboards came down and were followed by plaster, crumbling away from the walls in lumps and whole sheets. The great clock dropped from its fastening high on the wall, missed Old Gander's head by an inch, and spewed a tangle of springs and cogs over the heaving floor. The opaque glass in the door of the boys' coat-room sprang across the classroom, sailing over James' head, and went to pieces in a mighty splatter on the wall in front of him. The windows vanished, sashes and all. Not only the inner everyday windows, but the big storm-windows that were screwed on outside every Fall and taken off in the spring. The room, the big echoing school, the whole world, were filled with tremendous sound that came in waves, each visible in breakers of plaster dust.

Then the sound was gone, as suddenly as it had come, and in its place there was a srange and awful hush that was emphasized, somehow, by distant noises of falling plaster and tinkling glass. Grade Nine was on its feet, staring at Old Gander through a fog of plaster dust, and Old Gander stared back at them, with his scanty grey hair all on end, and his long seamed face the colour of snow when rain is turning it to slush. A waft of cold air came in from the street, where the windows should have been, and the fog cleared before it. A girl broke the silence, screaming shrilly. James perceived that her cheek was laid open from ear to mouth, with a great red river pouring down her chin, and that others were putting fingers to cut faces and heads, and staring strangely at the stains. Grade Nine was covered with plaster dust, and looked like a company of startled ghosts, and when James saw the thin red trickles running out of those white masks he knew he was dreaming, because things like that did not really happen. The girl with the red mask screamed again, and there was a chorus of screams, and then with one impulse the class turned and fled, as if it were Friday afternoon fire practice. James heard them clattering down the stairs into the street, with glass grinding and tinkling under their shoes. For a moment James was poised for similar flight, but in that moment he remembered the time he was frightened by a signboard groaning in the wind at night, and Dad's deep steady voice saying, "Never run from anything, son, till you've had a good look at it. Most times it's not worth running from."

Old Gander was standing beside his desk like a statue, staring at the lone survivor of his class. His watery blue eyes seemed awfully large. They looked like Mum's breakfast saucers. James moved jerkily towards him, licking plaster-dust from his lips. "What is it, Mister Burtle?" His own voice seemed queer and very far away, the way it sounded when you talked in your sleep and woke yourself up. Old Gander gazed at James in enormous surprise, as though he had never seen James before, as if James were speaking some foreign language not authorized by the School Board. Then he said in his old asthmatic voice, "James! Is that you, James?" and without waiting for a reply he added, as though it were the most ordinary thing in the world, "Some of the little boys have been playing with dynamite in the basement." James nodded slowly. Old Gander knew everything. The kids in the lower grades said he had eyes in the back of his head. He was a very wise old man.

They stood, silent, in the wrecked classroom for a space of minutes. Another gust of chill air stirred the thin hairs that stood out like a halo from the schoolmaster's head.

"You are a good boy, James," murmured Old Gander in a dazed voice. James squared his shoulders instinctively. After all, he was a sergeant in the school cadet corps. It was all right for the others to go if they wanted to. Old Gander passed a shaking hand back over his head, smoothing down the straggled hairs. Bits of plaster fell upon his dusty shoulders in a small shower, like a brittle sort of dandruff. "I think," he said vaguely, "we'd better see if there is any fire."

"Yes, sir," James said. It occurred to him that Mr. Burtle ought to look in the basement where the little boys had played with the dynamite. "I'll go through the upstairs classrooms, sir."

"Very good," murmured Old Gander, as if James were a superior officer. "I will search the lower floor and then the basement." And he added, "Don't stay up here very long, James." They separated.

James passed from room to room on the second floor. Each was like the one he had left, with blackboards tumbled off walls, heaps of plaster, doors hanging splintered in the jambs. Along the south side of the school the windows had disappeared into the street, but on the north side the shattered sashes were festooned over desks, and shards of glass in the tumbled plaster gave it the glitter of snow. The big assembly hall occupied most of the north side. Miraculously, the doors were still in place, but they refused to open. One was split badly in the panel, and James peeped through at a tangle of wood, piled against the doors on the inside. He thrust an arm through the hole and pushed some of the rubbish aside. The hall was a strange sight. The tall windows which occupied almost the entire north wall had come inwards, had swept across the hall, carrying chairs with them, and the shattered sashes had wedged against the south wall and the side doors in a complete barricade. There was no trace of fire.

James walked down the stairs, along the lower hall, and out through the main entrance into the snow. The stained glass that formerly cast a prism of colours from the transom over the great main door had gone outwards, and was littered over the snow in a jig-saw puzzle of many hues. Old Gander stood there in the snow amid the coloured fragments, staring up at the mute ruins of his school. James gave him a glance, no more. Something else had caught his eye. To the north-east, over the roofs of silent houses, a mighty mushroom was growing in the sky. The stalk of the mushroom was pure white, and it extended an enormous distance upward from invisible roots in the harbour; and at the top it was unfolding, spreading out rapidly in greasy curls, brown and black, that caught the December sun and gleamed with a strange effect of varnish. An evil mushroom that writhed slightly on its stalk, and spread its eddying top until it overshadowed the whole North End, strange and terrible and beautiful. James could not take his eyes from it.

Behind him a voice was speaking, a woman's voice that penetrated the mighty singing in his ears from a great distance. Miss M'Clintock, the Grade Seven teacher, arriving early for the day's work. She was a tall woman, masterful to the point of severity. There was a wild look on her face that astonished James; for he had spent a term under her much-libelled rule and had never seen her anything but calm and dignified. ". . . all along the street. I can't tell you what I've seen this morning. Are you listening to me, Mr. Burtle?" Old Gander removed his wide gaze from the ravaged building. "My first really modern school," he murmured in that quaint asthmatic falsetto. "Dear, dear. What will the School Board say?"

James was watching that poisonous fungus in the sky again, but something Miss M'Clintock was saying made him look towards the houses about the school. They were like the school, void of window-glass, and in some cases of doors as well. There

57

was a great silence everywhere, a dead quiet in which nothing moved except Old Gander and Miss M'Clintock and James and the mysterious mushroom that grew in the sky. But now over the whole city there came a great sigh, an odd breathless sound that was like a gasp and like a moan, and yet was neither. James saluted Old Gander awkwardly. "I — I guess I'd better go home now, sir." If Mr. Burtle heard him, he gave no sign. Miss M'Clintock said, "What a blessing the lower grades don't go in till half-past nine. All those big windows. Your hand is bleeding, James." James nodded and left them, walking out through the school gate and into the street.

Now there was a flurry of movement and a chorus of wild human sounds about the shattered houses. An oil wagon stood at the kerb, with a pair of great Percheron horses lying inert under the broken shaft. The teamster squatted beside them in the slush with his hands on their heads, addressing blood-stained people who scurried past without attention. "Dead!" he said to James in a queer surprised voice. "An' not a mark on 'em. Would you think a man could stand a Thing that killed a horse?" James began to run.

Home was not far up the street. The old brown house stood two hundred yards from the school. (Dad had said, "It'll be handy for the kids going to school. When I get back we'll look for something better.") Just now it was silent, without doors or windows. Ragged wisps of curtain dangled in the gaping window-frames fluttering with every stir of the December breeze like signals of distress. James went up the front steps shouting, "Mum! Mum!" The house was cold and still. Like a tomb. James ran, frantic, through that ominous quiet. Margery's room was empty, the bed littered with broken glass. Mum's room. His own room. Broken glass, crumbled plaster, shattered doors. Slivers of glass thrust like arrows through the panels of Margery's door. Bare laths where the plaster should have been, like the naked ribs of a skeleton. In the lower hall the long stove-pipe from the big anthracite heater lay in crumpled lengths, with soot mingled in the littered plaster, and the painting of Fujiyama that Dad brought home from a trip to the East was half-buried in the rubble, broken and forlorn. Confusion reigned, too, in the living-room; a window-sash, void of glass, was wedged against the piano, and the dusty mahogany was scored deep by invisible claws. In the wrecked kitchen he heard voices at last. Mum's voice, outside, in the garden. The rear door and the storm porch were lying, splintered, in the tiny scullery, amid a welter of broken chinaware and tumbled pots.

Mum's voice again, "James! Is that you, James?" James scrambled through the wreckage of the back door and ran into her arms, and they stood in the snow for several minutes, Mum and Margery and James, holding each other in silence. There was a bloody handkerchief about Mum's forehead, and little rivulets of blackish-red drying on her cheeks. Margery wore a coat over her nightdress.

Mum said, "I was looking out of the kitchen window, and suddenly across the way all the windows glowed red, as if they'd caught a gleam of sunset. Then our windows seemed to jump inwards." James said quickly, "Are you hurt, Mum?" but she shook her head. "Just cut a little about the forehead, I think, James. The window in Margery's room came right in on her bed, and she walked downstairs in her bare feet without a scratch. Over all that broken glass! It's a miracle, really."

"Why are you standing out here?" James demanded. It was cold, there in the snow without a coat. Mum waved her hand vaguely towards the street. "Somebody shouted, 'They're shelling the city — get behind your house!' So we came out here."

"I don't see how that could be," James considered gravely. "All the houses along the street are just like ours — doors and windows blown to pieces, and all the plaster down. The school, too. They couldn't do that. Not all at once, I mean."

There were sounds from next door. Old Mrs. Cameron appeared, embracing her husband in a strange hysterical way. He was breathing very heavily, for he was a fleshy man. Sweat

59

made little clean streaks in the grime of his face. Mr. Cameron was something in the railway.

"Station roof came down!" he shouted across to them. "All that steel and glass! Crawled out somehow! Ran all the way!" They came slowly to the garden fence, arms about each other, and Mum walked to meet them flanked by Margery and James.

"You hurt, Mrs. Gordon?" Mum shook her bandaged head again. "Nothing serious. Mr. Cameron, what does it all mean?" Mr. Cameron took an arm from his wife's waist and wiped his streaming face with a sleeve. "There was a terrible explosion in the harbour, down by the Richmond wharves. A munitions boat, they say. A French boat with two thousands tons of T.N.T. on board. She came up the harbour flying the red flag — the powder flag — and ran into another ship in the Narrows. She caught fire and blew up. It was like an earthquake. The whole North End of the city is smashed flat. Houses like bundles of toothpicks. And the boat went to pieces about the size of a plum — that big ship! When I ran up North Street the sky was raining bits of iron. I don't think many got out of the station alive."

Mum shivered. "No use standing here," James said. They went into the house and tramped silently through the shattered rooms. A motor-truck went past, soldiers leaning from the cab, shouting something urgent and incoherent. The street emerged from its dream-like silence for a second time that morning. Feet were suddenly splattering in the slush along the sidewalks, voices calling, shouting, screaming. Another truck went by, one of the olive-green army ambulances, going slowly. Soldiers hung from the doors, from the rear step, shouting up at the yawning windows. "What are they saying?" Mum said.

James said, "Sounds like, 'Get out of your houses.' " Mr. Cameron appeared on the sidewalk outside, shouting in to them through cupped hands. ". . . out! Magazine's on fire! Big magazine at the Dockyard! On fire!"

"Put on your coats and overshoes first," Mum said, her mouth in a thin white line. "Where's your coat, James?"

"In school," he mumbled, embarrassed. It was hanging in the coat-room, covered with plaster dust, like all the others, and he had run away forgetting everything, like the other kids after all. "Put on your old one," Mum said. Margery went upstairs, and after a few minutes came down again, dressed in a woollen suit. They went down the street steps together, and beheld a strange and tragic procession approaching from the direction of the city. Men, women, and children in all sorts of attire, pouring along the sidewalks, choking the street itself. Some carried suitcases and bundles. Others trundled hand-carts and perambulators laden with household treasures. Two out of three were bandaged and bloody, and all were daubed with soot and plaster. Their eyes glistened with an odd quality of fear and excitement, and they cried out to Mum as they stumbled past, "Get out! Out in the fields! There's another one coming! Dockyard's afire!"

Margery said, awed, "It's like pictures of the Belgian refugees." James looked at Mum's firm mouth and held his own chin high. They joined the exodus without words or cries. The human stream flowed westward. Every sidestreet was a tributary pouring its quota into the sad river. Open spaces began to appear between the houses, with little signboards offering "Lots for Sale." Then the open fields. The nearest fields were black with people already, standing in the snow with rapt white faces turned to the north-east, as in some exotic worship. The vanguard of the rabble halted uncertainly, like sheep confronted by a fence, and under the increasing pressure of those behind a great confusion arose. Their backs were to the stricken city. Before them lay the little valley of the Dutch Village Road, and beyond it the timbered ridges that cupped the city's water supply. Cries arose. "Here! Stop here!" And counter cries, "Too near! Move on!" At last someone shouted, "The woods! Take to the woods!" It was taken up, passed back from lip to lip. The stream moved on with a new pace, but Mum turned off the road into a field. They halted in a group of those strange expectant faces.

At the roadside was a pile of lumber. James went to the pile and pulled down some boards, made a small platform for Mum and Margery. Some of the people turned from their fearful gazing and said, "That's good. Better than standing in the snow." The lumber pile disappeared in a space of minutes. The great retreat poured past the field towards the Dutch Village Road for half an hour. Then it thinned, disintegrated into scattered groups, and was gone. The street was empty. The field was a human mass. Many of the women were in flimsy house-dresses, hatless and coatless. Two were clutching brooms in blue fingers. A blonde girl, with rouge-spots flaming like red lamps in her white cheeks, said, "Standing room only," with a catch in her voice. Nobody laughed. Most of the men were old. North-eastward rose fountains of smoke, black, white, and brown, merging in a great pall over the North End. The weird mushroom of those first tremendous minutes had shrivelled and disappeared in the new cloud. People watched the biggest of the black fountains. "That's the Dockyard," they said.

Two hours went by; long hours, cold hours. Still the people faced that black pillar of doom, braced for a mighty upheaval that did not come. There were more smoke fountains now, gaining in volume, creeping to right and left. A tall old man joined the crowd breathlessly, cried in a cracked voice. "The fire engines are smashed. The city is doomed." A murmur arose over the field, a long bitter sigh, like the stir of wind among trees. Someone said, "Nineteen days to Christmas," and laughed harshly. Three hours, and no blast from the burning Dockyard. Only the smoke poured up into the December sky. Old Mrs. Cameron came to them. She had become separated from her husband in the crowd and was weeping. "Joey! Joey!" she moaned, very softly. James thought this very strange. Joe Cameron had been killed at the Somme last year, and her other son's name was George. He was in France, too, in another regiment. But Mrs. Cameron kept moaning "Joey! Joey!" and wiping her eyes. She had no coat.

James said, "Looks as if we might be here a long time. I'll

go back to the house and get some blankets, and something to eat." Mum caught him to her swiftly. "No," she said, through her teeth. Surprisingly, old Mrs. Cameron said, "That's right, James. I'll go with you. Mrs. Gordon, you stay here with Margery." Margery was not well. James looked at Mum. "Anywhere outdoors we'll be just as safe as here. I won't be in the house very long." Mum stared at him queerly. "You sound like your father, James." They set off at a brisk pace, old Mrs. Cameron clutching his arm. The snow in the field had been packed to a hard crust under a thousand feet. Farther on, where the houses stood silent rows, it was like a city of the dead. Blinds and curtains flapped lazily in gaping window-frames. Clothing, silverware, all sorts of odds and ends were littered over hallways and doorsteps, dropped in the sudden flight. There were bloody hand-prints on splintered doors, red splashes on floors and entries. The slush on the sidewalks was tinged a dirty pink in many places, where the hegira had passed.

Home at last. Smoke curled, a thin wisp, from the kitchen chimney. It was absurd, that faithful flicker in the stove, when all the doors and windows were gone and the winter breeze wandered at will through the empty rooms. They paused outside for a moment. Old Mrs. Cameron said, "We must rush in and snatch up what we want. Don't stay longer than it takes to count a hundred. Remember, James." She moved towards her doorstep, drawing a deep breath. James nodded dumbly. He clattered up the steps, making a noise that seemed tremendous in the stark silence, then along the lower hall and upstairs, where his steps were muffled in fallen plaster. All the way he counted aloud. Numbers had a sudden and enormous significance. Margery's bed was full of broken glass, cumbered with wreckage of the window-sash. He stripped a blanket from his own bed and passed into Mum's room. Mum's big eiderdown was there on the bed. Her room faced south, and the window-glass had all blown out into the street. A gust of chill air came through the empty frame, and the bedroom door slammed shockingly. The interior doors had been open at the time of the great blast, and had suffered little injury. The slam gave James a sudden feeling of suffocation and made his heart beat terribly. He went to the door quickly and twisted the handle. It came away in his hand, and the handle on the other side fell with a sharp thud, taking the shaft with it. "Hundred-'n-ten, hundred-'n-'leven." James dropped his burden and tried to force back the catch with bits of wood. They splintered and broke, without accomplishment. Outside, old Mrs. Cameron was calling, "James! James!" her voice very loud in the awful silence. Fear came to James in a rush. He fancied that sidelong earthquake again, and the big brown house tumbling into the street, a bundle of toothpicks, as Mr. Cameron had said about the houses up Richmond way. He went to the window, and debated throwing the blankets into the street and jumping after them. It looked a terrible distance down there. Mrs. Cameron caught sight of him staring down at her, and waved her arms awkwardly and shouted. She had a blanket under each arm, a loaf of bread in one hand and a pot of jam in the other. Inspiration came to James at last. Dad's rifle kit. In the bottom drawer in Mum's big chiffonier. He snatched out the drawer, brought forth a tiny screwdriver, prised back the catch with it. Freedom! He came down the stairs in four leaps, dragging blanket and eiderdown, and was out in the street, sucking in an enormous breath. Old Mrs. Cameron scolded. "I thought you were never coming, James. You should have counted."

"I couldn't get out," James said. The breeze felt very cold on his brow. He put up a hand and wiped big drops of perspiration. As they approached the field again James stopped suddenly. "I forgot to get something to eat." He was very close to tears. Old Mrs. Cameron pulled at his arm. "I have bread and jam," she said. Mum and Margery were standing on the little wooden raft in the snow. Mum clutched James against her, and held him there a long time. It was two o'clock in the afternoon.

At half-past three an olive-green truck appeared from the city, stopped in the road by the field. Soldiers came. "Any badly injured here?" There were none. All the people in the field had walked there unaided. Most of them were bandaged roughly, but nobody wanted to go to the hospital. The hospital was in the city, too near that ominous pillar of smoke. Somebody said so. A soldier said, "It's all right now. You'd better go back to your homes. You'll freeze here. The magazine's all right. Some sailors went in and turned the cocks and flooded it." The truck roared away towards the city again. People stood looking at each other, with many side-glances at the smoke over burning Richmond. The old white-haired man wandered among them, shaking his bony fists at the smoke, a fierce exultation in his long face. "Woe unto ye, Sodom and Gomorrah! Alas, alas for Babylon, that mighty city! she shall be a heap." Old Mrs. Cameron muttered, "God have mercy." The girl with the rouge spots said, "You're getting your cities mixed, old man." A man cried, "Better to burn than freeze," and shouldering his bundle, walked off in the direction of the city, whistling "Tipperary." A few bold ones followed him. Then people began to move out of the field into the road in groups, walking slowly, cautiously, towards the city. The old man went with them, crying out in his wild voice. Nobody paid any attention.

Mum, James, and Margery got home at half-past four in the afternoon. Mr. Cameron was standing outside his house, staring up at the sky. The sunshine had vanished. The sky had turned grey, like steel. "It's going to snow," he said.

Mum said, "We'll have to spend the night in the kitchen." James looked at the kitchen stove-pipe. It was all right. He put coal on the faithful fire, and got the coal shovel out of the cellar and began to scoop plaster and broken glass from the kitchen floor, throwing it out into the snow. He counted the shovelfuls. There were seventy-five. "There's an awful lot of plaster in a room," Margery observed. Mum took a broom and swept up the fine stuff that escaped James' big shovel. They looked at the yawning window-frames. "That old storm-window," James said suddenly. "It's still in the cellar." They carried it up to the kitchen, and Mum and Margery steadied it while James mounted a table and drove nails to hold it in place of the vanished west window. It was meant to go on outside, of course, but there was no ladder, and it was terribly heavy. "We must have something to cover the other window," Mum said. They stared at each other. The people in the field had said you could not get glass or tarpaper in the city for love or money. James said, "The lumber—back in the field." Mum thought for a moment. "That lumber's gone by now, James. Besides, you couldn't carry a board all that way." They gathered up the living-room carpet, tugging it from under the tumbled furniture and shaking it clean of plaster. They folded it double and nailed it over the north window-frame on the inside, and James stuffed the gaps between nails with dish cloths and towels. There were two doors to the kitchen. The one opening into the lower hall had been open at the time of the explosion, and was unhurt. The other, opening into the shattered scullery, had been blown bodily off its lock and hinges. Mum and James pushed it back into place and wedged it there tightly with pieces of wood. "The snow will drift into the house everywhere," Mum said. "But we can't help that." James nodded soberly. "The water-pipes are going to freeze and burst." They debated nailing a carpet over the bathroom window. Finally Mum said, "The hall stove is out and the stove-pipe is down. The pipes will freeze whether we cover the windows or not. We must let the taps run and hope for the best. We can get help in the morning, I hope. To-night it's everyone for himself."

Through the makeshift storm-window they could see snow falling rapidly in the winter dusk. Mum made tea, and they ate bread and butter hungrily by the light of a candle. The stove created a halo of warmth about itself, but the rising wind began to whistle through the impromptu window coverings. Margery said, "Couldn't we go somewhere for the night?" Mum shook her head. "Everybody's in the same mess," James said. "Lots of the houses looked worse than ours." Mum looked at the fingers of fine snow that were growing along the kitchen floor under the windows. "We must keep the stove going, James." James carried chairs from the living-room, grouped them close about the stove, and stuffed a towel into the crack under the hall door. The candle on the kitchen table guttered blue in the cross draught from the windows. "Thirteen hours before we see daylight again," Mum whispered, as if to herself.

There was a knocking. James opened the hall door carefully, and saw the dim figure of a soldier framed in the front doorway, rapping knuckles against the splintered jamb. "Does James Gordon live here?" Mum stepped into the hall, shielding the candle with her hand. "Colonel James Gordon lives here. But he's — away, just now." The dim figure lifted a hand in a perfunctory salute. "I mean young James Gordon that goes to the big brick school down the street." James stepped forward, but Mum caught his shoulder firmly. "What do you want with James?" The soldier made as if to salute again, but took off his fur hat and ducked his head instead. He was a young man with a uniform far too big for him, and a long solemn face, rather sheep-like in the candle-light. "We — the sergeant, I mean — has been sent up to this here school for a — well, a special kinda job, ma'am. The awf'cer telephoned to the head schoolmaster's house. He lives 'way down in the city somewheres, but he said there was a boy named James Gordon lived handy the school an' would show us how to get in the basement, an' all like that."

James moved quickly, and Mum's hand slipped from his shoulder and fell to her side. "I won't be long, Mum." The soldier mumbled, "It's only a coupla hundred yards." Mum said, "Put on your coat and overshoes, James."

It was pitch dark, and the night was thick with snow. James led the way. The soldier plodded silently behind him. It was strange to be going to school at night, and the great silent building seemed very grim and awful with its long rows of black window-holes. A dark blur in the main doorway disintegrated, came towards them. Four men in fur hats and long flapping overcoats.

Soldiers. "You find the kid, Mac?" James' soldier said, "Yeah. This is him. Where's the sergeant?" One man waved a vague arm at the dim bulk of the school. "Scoutin' around in there some-wheres, lightin' matches. Tryin' to find the basement door." James said, "Which door do you want? You can get in the base-ment from the street if you like."

"Ah," grunted the second soldier; "that's the ticket, son."

A tiny point of light appeared within the school flickered down the stairs. James wondered why the sergeant looked upstairs for a basement door. A stout figure, muffled in a khaki greatcoat, was revealed behind the feeble flame of the match. The sergeant came out into the snow, swearing into a turned-up collar. With the shapeless fur hat on his head he looked strangely like a bear roused out of a winter den. "Here's the kid, Sarge." The sergeant regarded him. "Hello, son." James pointed. "The basement door is around there." He showed them. The door had been blown off its hinges and wedged, a bundle of twisted wood, in the frame. They pulled at the splintered wood stoutly, and the doorway was clear. On the basement steps the sergeant lit another match. Their voices echoed strangely in that murky cavern.

James knew them now for soldiers of the Composite Battal-ion, made up of detachments from various home-guard units. They wore the clumsy brown fur hats and hideous red rubber galoshes that were issued to the home guard for winter wear. Some people called them 'The Safety Firsts'; and it was com-mon for cheeky boys to hurl snowballs after their patrols from the shadow of alleyways, chanting —

"Com-Po-Zite!
They won't fight!"

Mum had cautioned James against such pleasantry. Some-body had to stay at home, and these men were mostly physical unfits, rejected by the overseas regiments.

"Big as all Hell," declared the sergeant, after a tour of the echoing basement. "Hold a thousand, easy." The soldiers said,

"Yeah." The sergeant fumbled in the big pockets of his great-coat and brought forth a dark bottle. He took a long swig, wiped his moustache with a sweep of mittened hand, and passed the bottle around. "Gonna be a cold job," he rumbled. "All the windows gone, an' snow blowin' in everywheres. Concrete floor, too." The sheep-faced soldier said, "What-say we tear up some floorboards upstairs an' cover some of these cellar winders?" The sergeant spat, with noise. "They gotta send up a workin' party from the Engineers if they want that done. We got dirty work enough." The soldiers nodded their hats again, and said "Yeah" and "Betcha life."

Wind swirled through the gloomy basement in icy gusts. The men leaned against the wall, huddled in their greatcoats, cigarettes glowing in the darkness. James walked up the concrete steps to street level and stood inside the doorway, staring into the snowy dark. He wondered how long he was supposed to stay. A glow-worm appeared down the street, a feeble thing that swam slowly through the whirl of snow towards the school. James experienced a sudden twinge of fright. There was a great white shape behind it. Then a voice from the darkness above that ghostly shape: "Hulloa!" James cleared his throat. "Hulloa!" A man rode up to the doorway on a white horse. A lantern dangled from the horse's neck, like a luminous bell. The rider leaned over, and a face became visible in the pale glow. He was a detective of the city police, and James recognized his mount as one of the pair that used to pull the Black Maria in the days before the war. He was riding bare-back, feet hanging down, and the big policeman looked very odd, perched up there. "Anyone else around, son?" James jerked his head towards the black hole of the basement entrance. "Some soldiers. Down there, sir. Do you want them?" The policeman turned his horse awkwardly. "Just tell 'em the first wagon will be right along." He kicked the glistening side of his mount and disappeared as silently as he had come, lantern a-swing. James shouted the message down into the darkness. "Okay!" There was a lull in the wind, and the bottle gurgled in the sudden stillness.

Another glow-worm came, as silent as the first. But as it turned in towards the school James caught a faint rattle of wheels, and a hoarse voice bellowed, "Whoa-hoa!" The soldiers came stumbling up the steps in the darkness, and James went with them towards the light. It was a wagon, one of the low drays that clattered along Water Street from morn to night. A man climbed stiffly from the seat. He was crusted with snow, even to his moustache and eyebrows. "Let's have the lantern, fella," demanded the sergeant. They walked to the back of the wagon, and the sheep-faced soldier held the lantern high while the sergeant whipped a long tarpaulin from the mysterious freight.

"Black men!" rumbled the sergeant loudly. James, peering between the soldiers in astonishment, beheld six figures lying side by side on the dray: three men, two women, and a young girl. They were stiff and impassive, like the dummies you saw in shop windows. The women had dirty rags of cotton dress. One of the men wore a pair of trousers. The rest were naked. Ebony flesh gleamed in the lantern light. The snowflakes drifted lightly on the calm up-turned faces. Their eyes were closed, hands lay easily at their sides, as if they were content to sleep there, naked to the storm. "Looka!" called the sheep-faced soldier. "They bin hit, Sarge. But there's no blood!" The sergeant stooped over for a better look. Two of the dark faces were scored deeply, as if some vandal had gouged wax from the dummies with a chisel. "Concussion," announced the sergeant with immense assurance. "That's what. Drives the blood inwards. They was dead before they got hit. That boat went to pieces like shrapnel." He called it "sharpnel.'

The teamster was complaining. ". . . get a move on, you guys. This snow gets much deeper I gotta go back to the barn an' shift to sleds. There's work to do." Two of the soldiers picked up a dummy by head and feet, carried it awkwardly down the basement steps, and dropped it. There was a dull 'flap' when it struck the concrete. They came up the steps quickly. "Froze?" asked Sarge. "Stiff as a board," they said. The wagon was cleared of its silent passengers and went away into the night. The sergeant struck matches while the men arranged the bodies in a neat row. "Once," a soldier said, "I worked in a meat packin' plant. In T'ronta, that was."

"Well," Sarge rumbled, "you're keeping your hand in."

Another lantern swam up the street, Another dray. More silent figures under the tarpaulin. White people this time. A man and four young women, nude, flesh gleaming like marble in the lantern light. There was blood, a lot of it, dried black like old paint. "Musta bin farther away," observed the sergeant. "Them black men was from Africville, right by the place she went off." T'ronta said curiously, "Funny, them bein' stripped this way. Was their clo'es blowed off, would you say?" The teamster shook his head. "Nuh. These was all pulled outa the wreckage by the troops this afternoon. Clo'es caught an' tore off, I guess. Besides, lotsa people sleeps late winter mornin's. Prob'ly didn't have much on, anyway." More wagons. The intervals diminished. The sheep-faced soldier said, "The awf'cer's forgot us. We oughta bin relieved by now." "Quit beefin'," said Sarge. "All the troops is up Richmond way, pullin' stiffs outa the wreckage, huntin' for livin' ones. If it's okay for them it's okay for us." A teamster gave them a spare lantern which they stood on the basement floor, and in the fitful glow of that lonely thing the dummies lay in orderly rows, toes up, faces towards the dim ceiling. The shadows of the soldiers performed a grotesque dance on the walls as they went about their work. Sarge pulled something from his greatcoat pocket, and James gave it a sidewise glance, expecting to see the bottle. Sarge thrust it back into the pocket again, but James had seen the silver figure of a baseball pitcher, and knew it had been wrenched from the big cup his school had won last summer. He said nothing. Sarge said, "You still here, son? We don't need you no more. Better go home."

Mum greeted James anxiously in the candle-lit kitchen. "How pale you are, James! What did they want? You've been gone three hours." James looked at the stove. "Nothing. Nothing much, Mum. I guess they — just wanted to fix up the school a bit." They sat in the cushioned chairs, huddling over the stove. Margery had her feet in the oven. James went upstairs and brought down blankets, and they muffled themselves up in the chairs. Mum said, "Don't you want something to eat, James? There's tea on the stove, and there's bread and butter." "Not hungry," James said in a low voice.

It was a long night. James had never known a night could be so long. Sometimes you would doze a little, and you would see the faces of the dead people on the drays as plain as anything. Then you would wake up with a start and find yourself sliding off the chair, and feeling terribly cold. Several times he took the hod and the candle down into the cellar and brought up more coal. When the candles burned down to the table he lit new ones and stuck them in the hot grease. After a while there was a pool of grease on the table, hard and wrinkled and dirty-white, like frozen slush in the street. Draughts came through the window-covers and under both doors, like invisible fingers of ice, and you had to keep your feet hooked in the rung of your chair, off the floor. The candles gave a thin blue light and made a continual fluttering sound, like the wings of a caged bird. Sometimes the house shook in the gusts, and twice James had to climb on the table and hammer more nails to keep the carpet in place. Snow drifted in between the carpet and the window-frame, and formed thin white dunes along the floor next the wall. The heat thrown off by the kitchen stove was lost between the bare laths of the walls and ceiling.

"There must be a lot of dead, poor souls," Mum said.

"Yes," James said.

"In the morning, James, you must go to the telegraph office and send a cable to your father. He'll be frantic."

"Yes," James said.

Mum had washed the blood from her face and tied a clean

72

rag of bedsheet over the cuts on her forehead. James thought she looked very white and hollow, somehow. But when he looked in her eyes there was something warm and strong in them that made him feel better. When you looked in Mum's eyes you felt that everything was all right. Margery had drawn a blanket over her head, like a hood, and her head was bent, hidden in the shadow. Mum said, "Are you awake, Margery?"

"Yes," Margery said quickly.

"Are you all right?"

"Yes."

"It will be morning soon," Mum said.

But it was a long time. They sat, stiff and cramped, over the stove, and listened to the snow sweeping into the rooms upstairs, and the flap-flap of broken laths, and blinds blowing to rags in the empty window-frames; and the night seemed to go on for ever, as though the world had come to a dark end and the sun would never come back again. James thought of Sarge, and the sheep-faced man, and T'ronta, carrying frozen dummies into the school basement, and wondered if the awf'cer had remembered them. Daylight crept through the storm-window at last, a poor grey thing that gave a bleak look to everything in the kitchen. Stove, blankets — nothing could ward off the cold then. The grey light seemed to freeze everything it touched. Outside, the snow still swept fiercely against the carpet and the glass. James found potatoes in the cellar, and rescued bacon and eggs from the wreck of the pantry. Mum brushed the snow and bits of plaster from the bacon and put it in a frying-pan. It smelt good.

The telegraph office was full of people waving bits of scribbled paper. The ruins of plate-glass windows had been shovelled out into the street, and the frames boarded up. Outside, a newsboy was selling papers turned out by some miracle on battered presses in the night. They consisted of a single sheet, with "HALIFAX IN RUINS" in four-inch letters at the top. Within the telegraph office, lamps cast a yellow glow. There was a great buzz of voices and the busy clack-clack of instruments. James

73

had to wait a long time in the line that shuffled past the counter. A broad cheerful face greeted him at last.

"What's yours, son?"

"I want to send a cable to Colonel James Gordon, in France."

The man leaned over the counter and took a better look at him. "Hello! Are you Jim Gordon's son? So you are. I'd know that chin anywhere. How old are you, son?"

"Four — going on fifteen," James said.

"Soon be old enough to fight, eh? What's your Dad's regiment?"

James paused. "That'll cost extra, won't it?" he suggested shrewdly. "Everybody in the army knows my father."

The man smiled. "Sure," he agreed reasonably. "But France is a big place, son. It's their misfortune, of course, but there's probably a lot of people in France don't know your Dad."

James said, "It's the Ninetieth."

"Ah, of course. Jim Gordon of the Ninetieth. There's an outfit will keep old Hindenburg awake nights, son, and don't you forget it. What d'you want to say?"

James placed both hands on the counter. "Just this: 'All's well. James Gordon.' That's all."

The man wrote it down, and looked up quickly. "All's well? That counts three words, son, at twenty-five cents a word. Why not just, "All well'?"

James put his chin up. "No. 'All's well.' Send it like that."

Barometer Descending

Terry Crawford

the seance was a dream
by an ancient fireplace
your   eyes   spoke
of a living tree
waving in God's breath
the vision was a calm sea
    and
a single white citadel
the high hustle of a child
swinging in a green yard
was instantly photographed
by a howling flash
that fired the heavens

    when the seance burned down
    the visitation was announced
    100,000 souls in Halifax
    know the exquisite wind
    of ten megatons fallen
    off the lap of god

Jerome

Joan Balcom

A legless mystery man called 'Jerome' lived, almost sixty years, along the inland bend on the Fundy Shore of Nova Scotia known as St. Mary's Bay. Yet, to this day, no one knows . . . for sure, from where he came, or why.

Who the stranger was or why his mutilated body was cast up, one day, on the sandy shore of St. Mary's Bay has been kept a closely guarded secret during more than a century of time. But those who knew him well believed he was of royal blood . . . cast out on that sparsely populated shore because of some misdeed in an age when punishment was often quick, cruel and unrelenting.

When fishermen first found the man they called Jerome he was a legless, speechless man. Yet, the old folks say that, even then, there was an aura of regal dignity about the pitiful figure. Some say he was a king stricken from his European homeland. Others are sure he was a high-ranking officer of an European court. Whatever Jerome's secret was . . . it remains a secret still.

Jerome was first sighted by a simple fisherman known as George Albrite. Albrite lived on the north side of St. Mary's Bay near the village of Sandy Cove. It is said that he was gathering rockweed along the shore at Sandy Cove one day, when he noted a strange figure lying prone against the only rock in sight. He hurried for a closer look. Salt water from the sparkling Bay

76

licked at a man's body as the incoming tide swelled those heavy waters.

At first sight, Albrite believed the man to be dead. He examined the body more closely and was alarmed to discover the still figure had no legs. His breathing was scarcely audible above the murmur of the tide.

Both the stranger's legs had been severed at the knees. Beyond that, the man's body appeared intact. A youthful figure, this stranger had blond hair, blue eyes and a noble face which brought quick compassion for his plight.

The simple fisherman stooped quickly ... He felt the texture of the man's navy blue suit. The coat was dry. The style was strange to the fisherman and felt rich to his touch. George Albrite knew for certain that this man had not swum in from the Bay for his clothing was not wet. There was no salt crusted from dried sea water about the seams. Someone had surely placed this legless mystery man by the Cove's big rock.

Albrite looked quickly about the still beach. He turned troubled eyes to the churning sea. There was no one in sight. Only the water moved, and light clouds as they flowed overhead. Along all that beach, as far as the eye could see, only the huge boulder and the legless mystery man broke the flatness of the sand. A tin box of biscuits and a can of fresh water were near the man's hand.

It was then that the man called Albrite recalled the strange ship which had sailed up these quiet waters of St. Mary's Bay on the previous night's tide. It had been an European war ship, appearing sinister and unfamiliar to the old fisherman's eyes. Albrite shivered inside his heavy clothing. He recalled watching that strange ship until darkness closed in over the Bay as it moved quietly just off Digby Neck.

Now it was noon. A bright sun shone overhead. No vessel broke the rhythm of the tide. There was only the crude fisherman and the still form of the legless mystery man.

Turning quickly, Albrite hurried along the beach to the village for help. It was not long before gentle hands lifted that unconscious form from the water's edge. The villagers carried the stranger to the Sandy Cove home of a Mr. Samuel Gidney.

Friendly villagers laid the legless stranger on a padded couch. As his outer garments were removed, the fishermen marvelled at the richness of the blue serge suit. Never before had they seen clothing the like of this. The stranger wore a shirt of heavy satin and undergarments of pure silk. In their excitement at finding this mysterious man, it was some time before the fisher-folk realized that every button had been cut from the suit. His pockets were empty. There was no indication of from where the man had come.

The villagers whispered amongst themselves. And, all this time, the stranger did not utter a single sound. He lay quietly in the fisherman's house with staring eyes that seemed not even aware of the fervour around him.

As the days passed, the mystery grew.

Men and women from throughout the village visited the Gidney home. To all of them the mystery man was as strange as were his clothes. They examined the stranger's coat and trousers, and all other of his articles of clothing and not a single identifying mark was found. Who was this man? they wondered. From where did he come... and why?

It was during the summer of 1864 that Jerome was first found on the sandy beach. The doctor that tended him claimed the stranger's legs had been skillfully removed in the fashion of a surgeon. No reason, except for shock, could be found for the man's mute state.

The villagers were a kindly people. They carefully tendered the stranger's amputated legs. Warm broths were made by the women and, soon, the man began to eat.

As the warm days of summer stole by, faint color crept into the man's face to brighten the pallor of ill health. The stranger ate when fed and slept, fitfully, on the cot provided for him in the Gidney home. But ... in all that time, he did not smile. He showed no recognition of his new-found friends.

Weeks went by, and still the mysterious man had not uttered a single word.

Then, one day, a neighbour-woman of French descent was in the house for tea. While tending to the stranger, she heard him make a sound. The word he uttered was scarcely audible but sounded like "Jerome". So it was that, from that day, the mystery man was known, throughout the region, as Jerome.

It is said that the kindly neighbour-woman talked to Jerome for a long time that day. But, try as she would, not another word passed the man's dry lips.

The villagers' concern grew. Perhaps Jerome understood French.

They soon decided to move their strange friend into the home of John Nicholas at Meteghan. Nicholas was a corsican who spoke several languages. He welcomed Jerome into his home and watched him closely those first few weeks. It was not long before Nicholas was certain Jerome understood both French and Italian. But, still, he would not speak.

Jerome lived with his Fundy friends almost sixty years. It is said that in all that time he uttered only three words and that each time he was made to speak he would becomed enraged, in a mute anger which lasted for days.

One day, Nicholas turned quickly to Jerome and asked ... in French, the name of the stranger's homeland. The old folks say Jerome whispered the word "Trieste", then became very angry and mumbled in a language which not even Nicholas could understand.

Jerome lived with John Nicholas some seven years until the old Frenchman's death. Then he was moved into the nearby Acadian cottage of Didier Comeau at St. Alphonse where he lived some forty-five years with the French people of Nova Scotia. News of the mystery man spread throughout the land. It was not long before the government of the country also became concerned for the legless man's plight, and supported him with an annual grant of $104.00 for 'bed and board'.

The villagers' curiosity remained unsated. So it was that, year after year, they continued to question Jerome. One day his friends demanded to know the name of Jerome's ship. To their surprise, Jerome said 'Colombo'. Then ... his lips closed tightly, his face grew livid with anger while inaudible sounds surged from his throat, and he refused to utter another word.

Except when provoked into speaking, Jerome was a quiet man. It is said that he was "almost shy" when in the presence of adults. It was when the children of the village came to call that Jerome appeared most at ease. His eyes would take on a new light and his gaunt frame visibly relax as he patted the towsled head of a small Acadian boy.

Jerome had made his home with Didier Comeau for many years when, one day, a strange car entered the Acadian village. Driven by a uniformed chauffeur, it carried ladies and bore the license of an American State.

The car drove straight to the house of Didier Comeau. Speaking fluent French, the ladies asked for the "deaf man" who resided there. As the ladies entered the Acadian cottage, curious villagers flocked about the door. They noted that these new strangers were elegantly dressed. Both their clothing and their stately carriage appeared strange and unfamiliar to the eyes of those simple fishers.

It was not long before the ladies had closeted themselves with Jerome in his modest quarters. They remained there, behind closed doors, for several hours. Didier Comeau could hear them talking and strained his ears to listen. It was apparent Jerome was taking an active part in the strange conversation. Didier leaned nearer the door. He could hear them talking clearly but the language those people spoke was strange to him.

After the visitors had departed, Jerome remained closeted in his room for a long time. He neither spoke nor ate, and

80

showed no sign of what had transpired during that mysterious visit.

Like the strange visitors, Jerome himself had the carriage of one born of nobility. It is said that in almost sixty years there were only rare occasions when Jerome appeared caught off-guard. With eyes staring unseeingly across the room, he seemed to ignore the hum of conversation around him unless someone spoke the word 'traitor'. At this, Jerome would invariably go into a blazing rage which often lasted for several days.

The villagers continued to watch and question Jerome. They were certain he could read and understand a number of languages including French, English, Italian and German. While recounting tales of the mystery man, the old folks say Jerome often sat with a book in his lap. He would hold the book in an upsidedown position and appear to stare blindly at a printed page. Then, when it seemed no one was watching, Jerome would revert the book to its proper position and become momentarily absorbed in reading the printed words... regardless of the origin of the book or the language used in it.

Villagers often tell of Didier Comeau's son Charles, and the visit this youth made to New York in search of work. It is said that Charles was visited by two strange ladies while in the great city. They claimed to know Jerome, saying that Nova Scotia's mystery man's name was Mahoney and that they had known him in Alabama.

The ladies gave Charles a sealed letter without name or address and asked that he present it to Jerome on his return. Charles delivered the letter as requested and saw a strange thing happen. Jerome took the envelope in both hands. He turned the paper this way and that with no sign of emotion then, turning quickly, fed the envelope into the flickering flames above the hearth.

Along the Fundy Shore, the mystery of Jerome grew with each passing year. But still, Jerome kept his silent role all the while he made his home with the kindly villagers at St. Alphonse. And so... the mystery is there still.

Jerome died at St. Alphonse on April 19, 1912. No stone marks his resting place in the Catholic cemetery at Meteghan but Acadians along the Fundy shore can quickly point to his burial spot. Along the northern coast of St. Mary's Bay the huge boulder near which the fishermen first sighted their mystery man remains there still. It is known to this day, as the "Jerome Rock".

Who was Jerome?

No secret was ever kept so well as this. The mystery man lived some fifty-eight years amongst the Acadian French-Canadian people in Nova Scotia. Even though they knew him well, they knew him not at all.

And in all the years since the mysterious man's death no truth has yet been learned to solve the strange enigma. Folks along the Fundy Shore often talk of the 'legless mystery of Meteghan'. They wonder, still, from Where he came . . . and Why.

Caribou standing in snow

George Jones

Collected by Dr. Helen Creighton

1. Good people all, come listen to my melancholy tale,
   My dying declaration which I have penn'd in jail.
   My present situation may to all a warning be,
   And a caution to all seamen to beware of mutiny.

2. George Jones is my name, I am from the county Clare,
   I quit my aged parents and left them living there.
   I being inclined for roving, at home I would not stay,
   And much against my parents' will I shipped and went to
      sea.

3. My last ship was the *Saladin*, I shudder at her name,
   I joined her in Valparaiso on the Spanish Main.
   I shipped as cabin steward which proved a fatal day,
   A demon came aboard of her which led us four astray.

4. I agreed to work my passage, the ship being homeward
      bound,
   With copper ore and silver and over thousand pounds;
   Likewise two cabin passengers on board of her did come,
   The one was Captain Fielding, the other was his son.

5. He did upbraid our captain before we were long at sea,
   And one by one seduced us into a mutiny;
   The tempting prize did tempt his eyes, he kept it well in view,
   And by his consummate art he's destroyed us all but two.

6. On the fourteenth night of April I am sorry to relate,
   We began his desperate enterprise—at first we killed the
      mate;
   Next we killed the carpenter, and overboard him threw,
   Our captain next was put to death with three more of the
      crew.

7. The watch were in their hammocks when the work of death
       begun,
   The watch we called, as they came up we killed them one by
       one;
   These poor unhappy victims lay in their beds asleep,
   We called them up and murdered them, and hove them in
       the deep.

8. There were two more remaining still below and unprepared,
   The hand of God protected them that both their lives were
       spared;
   By them we're brought to justice and both of them are free.
   They had no hand in Fielding's plan, nor his conspiracy.

9. An oath was next administered to the remainder of the crew,
   And like a band of brothers we were sworn to be true.
   This was on Sunday morning when the bloody deed was
       done,
   When Fielding brought the Bible and swore us every one.

10. The firearms and weapons all we threw into the sea,
    He said he'd steer for Newfoundland, to which we did agree,
    And secret all our treasure there in some secluded place;
    If it was not for his treachery that might have been the case.

11. We found with Captain Fielding (for which he lost his life)
    A brace of loaded pistols, likewise a carving-knife;
    We suspected him for treachery which did enrage the crew;
    He was seized by Carr and Galloway and overboard was
        threw.

12. His son exclaimed for mercy, as being left alone,
    But his entreaties were soon cut off, no mercy there shown.
    We served him like his father was who met a watery grave,
    So we buried son and father beneath the briny wave.

13. Next it was agreed upon before the wind to keep,
    We had the world before us then, and on the trackless deep;
    We mostly kept before the wind as we could do no more,
    And on the twenty-eighth of May we were shipwrecked on
        the shore.

14. We were all apprehended, and into prison cast,
    Tried and found guilty, and sentence on us passed,
    Four of us being condemned and sentenced for to die,
    And the day of execution was the thirtieth of July.

15. Come, all you pious Christians, who God is pleased to spare,
    I hope you will remember us in your pious prayer;
    Make appeals to God for us, for our departing souls.
    I hope you will remember us when we depart and mould.

16. Likewise the pious clergymen, who for our souls did pray,
    Who watched and prayed along with us, whilst we in prison
        lay;
    May God reward them for their pains, they really did their
        best,
    They offered holy sacrifice to God to grant us rest.

17. And may the God of mercy, who shed His blood so free,
    Who died upon the holy cross all sinners to set free.
    We humbly ask His pardon for the gross offence we gave,
    May He have mercy on our souls when we descend the
        grave.

18. We were conveyed from prison, unto the gallows high,
    Ascended on the scaffold, whereon we were to die.
    Farewell, my loving countrymen, I bid this world adieu,
    I hope this will a warning be to one and all of you.

19. They were placed upon the fatal drop, their coffins beneath
        their feet,

And their Clergy were preparing them, their Maker for to
    meet;
They prayed sincere for mercy, whilst they humbly smote
    their breast,
They were launched into eternity, and may God grant them
    rest.

No. 2 in the group of songs of the *Saladin* mutiny, which are
the last dying thoughts of three of the four men hanged for murder in Halifax. In an issue of the *Acadian Recorder* of 1924 "Occasional" tells that they were composed by a fisherman, and
suggested by the confession of the men. "Mr. Forhan saw the
four men hanged. He was six years old at the time. His father
and mother and he stood on the spot where the Victoria General
Hospital now stands, and saw the two wagons come from the
penitentiary. They were surrounded by a squad of soldiers with
fixed bayonets. They came up Tower Road, and when they
arrived the wagons turned in west and when 200 yards from the
spot where the gallows were erected, the troops formed a circle
around it. This was the exact spot, and after they dropped we
started for home, and on top of the citadel, looking back, saw
the heads of the four men still hanging on the gallows." The
Saladin muntiny took place in 1844.

Song of the Tangier Gold Mines

Catherine Hart

1. Oh, in eighteen hundred and sixty-one,
   All in the month of May,
   When Nova Scotia was very poor,
   As I ofttimes heard them say;
   But since I've got the secret,
   A story I'll unfold,
   Back of Tangier and Pope's Harbour
   Where they're digging out the gold,

2. It's all through the country,
   Those golden veins do run;
   And those who have not much to do
   They only think of fun,
   With their pick upon their shoulder,
   And their shovel in their hand,
   Seeking out the golden veins
   Among the rocky land.

3. There are farmers and fishermen,
   Likewise sailors too;
   Blacksmiths and shoe-makers
   Among the jovial crew.
   Carpenters and shop-keepers,
   As I've been lately told,
   All leave their wives and sweethearts
   For the sake of "Tangier gold."

4. Just go up on the diggings,
   If you'll not believe me;
   And walk up through Gold Street,
   It's there you soon shall see —
   The houses they are building,

88

And the trees they have cut down;
And in the course of eighteen months,
I guess they'll have a town.

5. They have crushing pans and horses too,
   For them who take the lead;
   Their houses shall all be furnished well
   With everything they need.
   They shall all live in splendour,
   Those hearts that are so bold;
   For their precious lives they venture
   For the sake of Tangier gold.

6. If the gold does turn out plenty,
   How rich the folks will be;
   Their houses won't be empty,
   Of molasses, flour or tea,
   Rum, sugar and tobacco,
   And all other things in store.
   Success attend the miners,
   It's a blessing to the shore.

7. If you happen to get rich,
   Now of it make good use.
   Don't lie, steal or murder,
   Your neighbours don't abuse.
   Don't spend your gold in drunkenness,
   You'll find it is a sin;
   But try and build a larger church,
   Let all the folk get in.

8. If you meet a poor widow,
   Let her be young or old,
   See you don't molest her,
   But bestow on her some gold.
   And if you give it freely

89

You'll have good luck, you know,
For relieving the poor widow,
Who was in the midst of woe.

9. A verse about the ladies now,
   I'm sure there ought to be;
   They go upon the diggings,
   The miners for to see.
   Some they are acquainted with,
   And others they don't know;
   There's one young lady fell in love
   With California Joe.

10. Now, here's to the miners!
    To them I do suppose
    Digging gold, it is hard work,
    That all of them well know.
    And should you wish to marry,
    Don't lead a single life,
    And do no longer tarry,
    But present yourself a wife.

11. Now if my song displeases you,
    I'm sure I'm not to blame;
    It was not made to tease you,
    For I speak no person's name.
    I only have composed it
    To make your work go light.
    And those who can peruse it
    May pass away the night.

12. And now my song is ended,
    I have no more to sing;
    And to the one who made it,
    Give gold to make a ring.
    And to a child who sings it,

Of sweeties — give it some;
But of a man, of your own clan,
He deserves a drink of rum.

13. And now my jolly miners,
    I wish you all success;
    And the one who has composed this song,
    'Twill puzzle them to guess.

Note from Archives at Halifax: "The Tangier Gold Mines opened in 1860. The district covers 30 square miles and has 12 lodes of auriferous quartz. The ground is honeycombed with pits and shafts for miles. Gold was not found in quantities, but lucrative shore-workings were engaged in for some time..." Unfortunately it has never been as lucrative as the dreams of the composer of this song. California Joe, mentioned in v. 9, is the hero of a song by that name.

— *Collected by Dr. Helen Creighton*

Evangeline

Chant Acadien
Affectueusement dedie a nos freres
les Acadiens Paroles et musique de
A. T. Bourque

1. Je l'avais cru, ce rêve du jeune âge,
   Qui, souriant, m'annonçait le bonheur,
   Et confiante en cet heureux présage,
   Mes jeunes ans s'écoulaient sans douleur.
   Il est si doux, au printemps de la vie,
   D'aimer d'amour les amis de son coeur,
   De vivre heureux au sein de la Patrie,
   Loin du danger, à l'abri du malheur,
   Loin du danger, à l'abri du malheur.

Refrain:

   Evangeline, Evangeline,
   Tout chante ici ton noble nom;
   Dans le vallon, sur la colline,
   L'echo repete et nous repond:
   Evangeline, Evangeline.

2. Qu'ils étaient beaux, ces jours de notre enfance,
   Cher Gabriel, au pays de Grand-Pré,
   Car là régnaient la paix et l'innocence,
   Le tendre amour et la franche gaiete;
   Qu'ils étaient doux, le soir sous la charmille,
   Les entretiens du village assemblé!
   Comme on s'aimait!
   Qu'elle aimable famille
   On y formait sous ce ciel adoré,
   On y formait sous ce ciel adoré.

Refrain:

3. Là, les anciens, devisant du ménage,
   Avec amour contemplaient leurs enfants
   Qui réveillaient les échos du village
   Par leurs refrains et leurs amusements.
   La vie alors coulait douce et paisible
   Au vieux Grand-Pré, dans notre cher pays,
   Lorsque soudain, notre ennemi terrible
   Nous abreuva de malheurs inouis.

Refrain:

4. Hélas! depuis, sur la terre étrangere,
   J'erre toujours en proie à la douleur,
   Car le destin dans sa sombre colère
   M'a tout ravi, mes amis, mon bonheur.
   Je ne vois plus l'ami de mon enfance
   A qui j'avais juré mon tendre amour,
   Mais dans mon coeur je garde l'espérance
   De le revoir dans un meilleur séjour.

Refrain:

Partons
La Mer Est Belle!

Folklore Acadien

1. Amis, partons sans bruit;
La pêche sera bonne,
La lune qui rayonne
Eclairera la nuit.
Il faut qu'avant l'aurore
Nous soyons de retour,
Pour sommeiller encore
Avant qu'il soit grand jour.

Refrain:

Partons, la mer est belle;
Embarquons-nous, pêcheurs,
Guidons notre nacelle,
Ramons avec ardeur.
Aux mâts hissons les voiles,
Le ciel est pur et beau:
Je voisbriller l'étoile
Qui guide les matelots!

2. Ainsi chantait mon père,
Lorsqu'il quitta le port,
Il ne s'attendait guère
A y trouver la mort.
Par les vents, par l'orage,
Il fut surpris soudain.
Et d'un cruel naufrage
Il subit le destin.

Refrain:

3. Je n'ai plus que ma mère

Qui ne possède rien;
Elle est dans la misère,
Je suis son seul soutien.
Ramons, ramons bien vite,
Je l'aperçois là-bas;
Je la vois qui m'invite
En me tendant les bras.

Refrain:

Giant MacAskill

from Lightly

Chipman Hall

Grandad and I started to walk up the island towards the mouth of the cove. There is a little path that runs up to about opposite the government wharf, and then a sandy beach running around to a point almost on the far side of the island. Grandad walked ahead of me on the path. He walked at my pace. Before, in the earlier times when he came back, I always remember having to run to keep up.

I loved the sand beach and never was there without taking my shoes off. Many of the kids would never do that. Today I had to carry them with me because we weren't going to come back this way. We were going all the way around. I was ahead of Grandad up to the point. He walked strongly and as straight as the trees he said he was like.

The point has hundreds of good flat rocks, good for skipping. I could often make fifteen long skips if the bay was pretty calm. Hit off the top of the first wave and they really go. After I threw some really far ones, I went up and sat next to Grandad. He was seated on one of the two stones on the edge of the beach that are almost formed like low chairs. People are always sitting on them.

"You see that big rock that looks like half an egg over there."

"Yes."

"How did it get there, Bayo. Do you know."

"No."

"It was the Giant MacAskill who skipped it there from Bush Island right to out there. Seeing you skipping stones put me in mind of it. No one has told you before."

"No. How."

Storytelling must be serious work to Grandad because right away he sets his face into a look I see all the time when he is about to have me listen to him. His eyes don't see me anymore at first, as though he has taken them inside to bring the story out, and then they come back to see it out in front of him, where eyes are supposed to be seeing. After he's well started into the story, he begins to look as if he is the best listener to it. I would like to look like Grandad waiting to hear how his own story is going to turn out.

"I heard the story many years ago. The Giant MacAskill from Cape Breton had become so famous for his strength that another giant from the west called Billium Moore came to find him to see who was the strongest. They went up and down Nova Scotia. Some say they even went down to New York, trying feats of strength.

"Now they came to this very point because in those days there used to be good skipping stones the size of about four lobster traps set side by side.

"Well, they started skipping those, but it wasn't much of a feat for them. So they said they should try to skip them over Bush Island, and after a few tries they both could do that. The problem was to find something more difficult. And then they saw it. On the end of Bush Island was a rock the shape of a giant egg, about twelve feet high and fifteen feet long. Only a whale could have been big enough to make an egg that size."

"But whales don't lay eggs."

97

"Nowadays they don't. So Billium Moore says, 'I'll break that egg in two and then we'll see who can skip it clear over to the point,' Briar Point there. Giant MacAskill agrees, and they go out to the island. Billium picks up the rock but it's too big for him to break. Then MacAskill says he better do it. But to tell the truth, it was too much even for him. So the two of them heft it up together and bang it end down on that rock ledge, which used to be much larger, and they cleave it perfectly in half, from end to end.

"Then MacAskill, who was a great gentleman as well as a giant, invites Billium Moore to go first. This was Billium's idea so he was hard up with himself about winning. Now, I'll tell you never had any man put so much strength into skipping a rock. He lifts her up, gets it real steady so the flat side will hit the water smack on. And he throws it with such might that the wind from the stone nearly blew MacAskill over as it shoots past him. It hits the water exactly as he wants and so solid it turns the wave that shoots out from under it into steam, and this time nearly boiled MacAskill as it drenched down over him.

"Billium knew what he was doing. Each time the stone hits the water it makes such heat that it's almost exploded on further. And all the time the rock is getting hotter and hotter, till finally it's almost to the shore, and it hits down on the water again. Only this time the water is too shallow to take all the mighty heat, and it just evaporates all away underneath so the rock hits the bottom, and in an instant with the heat of it hitting the solid bottom, Billium's rock breaks in three and can do no more than roll up to the edge of the shore.

"Still, with the water sizzling around the three great pieces, Billium isn't worried and he says to the Giant MacAskill, 'You darn't have to try to beat that if you want to save your strength.'

"Only Giant MacAskill weren't all that worried. He knew more about the sea than Billium, and he knew how he was going to try to outdo Billium's feat.

"The Giant picks up his half of the great egg. But he holds the flat side up in the air, with the rounded side down and the narrow end forward, like the hull of a boat. Also, he holds it underarm so he can shoot her out straight as an arrow in flight. Now he watches the waves rolling up onto Briar Point.

"In those days every seventh wave was the biggest, that's why seven is a magic number. He waits until a seventh wave is about to roll ashore over Billium's pieces. Then Giant MacAskill launches his rock with a mighty heave, and it goes streaming through the air till it hits the water just over the crest of a seventh wave that's rolling in there from the Atlantic. And the Giant's rock goes surging down into the trough like a clipper ship in a following sea and a 40-knot breeze on her stern quarter. Now the hull shape of the stone lifts her like a boat and she comes surging out of the trough and rides over the wave tops until she hits the next seventh. And that's the way Giant MacAskill's rock rode the sea all the way into the shore. And just as she was slowing down and Billium was certain it was going to flounder on the great pieces of his rock, Giant MacAskill's rock boat catches the last seventh wave and rides up onto the beach over top of Billium's trap. And that's how I always heard that great rock got to be sitting there on Briar Point."

"Have you ever done anything like that."

"No. Giant MacAskill and men like Billium Moore were pretty exceptional, and you don't seem to see any more like them now."

"What happened to them."

"Well, Billium went back west and never seemed to feel quite so strong, and after awhile we never heard of him anymore. Giant MacAskill died some years later in New York. He was getting a little older and one day he picked up a great anchor and was going to throw it to show his strength, but he didn't raise it high enough and the shank caught him in his back and I guess it pierced through into his lungs and killed him."

That left me silent a moment. Then I decided I'd think about it later 'cause I wanted to keep Grandad talking.

"Do you know how everything got to be around here, Grandad."

"Oh, I've heard of a lot of stories up and down the coast, and I've learned a fair bit from the sea herself."

"Can you learn about people from the ocean."

"Sure you can, and she'll teach you about yourself first off. Once you've come to know somewhat who you are, then the ocean has you well set to know some of the important things about other people, about what makes us good or what keeps us from being as good to ourselves and others as we would like to be."

The Gods War Over a Golden Apple and Troy Falls All Over Again

Gregory M. Cook

"You know where Northern Spies come from, don't you?"
Asks the vet whose chaplain taught The Golden Rule,
and whose officers taught, "Kill your enemies."
So he joined the medical corps of his own conscience.
"You know where Northern Spies come from?"
He asks his favorite beerhall table.

"Well, they didn't find out until before the last war.
It was before the first war these fellas —
They came off ships in Halifax and around —
Went to the Valley with these apple tree roots,
like peddlers, selling them to small farmers
On the North Mountain and on the South Mountain."

"Well, it was after the first, before the second war,
they discovered these fellas weren't just peddlers.
They were surveyors from Germany, you see.
Yeah, they'd peddle their yellow apples
on the North Mountain and on the South Mountain.
That's how we got these apples, Northern Spies."

"Yeah, after the last war people liked red apples,
so they was a cross with Northerns and we got Red Spies.
Oh, yeah. You research it. It's documented somewhere."
Another round of beer is ordered for the listeners
who decide the story of yellow apples made red
is true, even if it never happened.

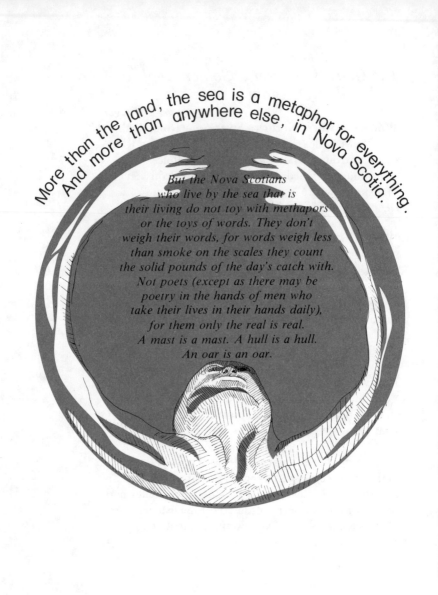

More than the land, the sea is a metaphor for everything.
And more than anywhere else, in Nova Scotia.

But the Nova Scotians
who live by the sea that is
their living do not toy with methapors
or the toys of words. They don't
weigh their words, for words weigh less
than smoke on the scales they count
the solid pounds of the day's catch with.
Not poets (except as there may be
poetry in the hands of men who
take their lives in their hands daily),
for them only the real is real.
A mast is a mast. A hull is a hull.
An oar is an oar.

Sailmaker

Bill Howell

Late tonight with canvas
and tight twine he reefs
and reams his ageless light.

Upstairs his sons sleep
close with their wives and
latest plans for leaving.

His time and tomorrow's tide
will slide them all away
on seas of wind where maybe
they'll believe the best
of his billowing dreams.

Halibut Cove Harvest

Kenneth Leslie

The kettle sang the boy to a half-sleep;
and the stir, stir of the kettle's lid
drummed a new age
into the boy's day-dream.
His mind strove with the mind of steam
and conquered it
and pressed it down and shaped it
to the panting giant
whose breath lies heavy on the world.

This is a song of harvest;
the weather thickens with a harsh wind
on this salt-seared coast;
offshore a trawler, smoke-smearing the horizon,
reaps the sea.

Here on the beach
in the cove of the handliner
rain flattens the ungathered dulse,
and no cheek reddens to the rain.
From the knock-kneed landing
a faltering path is lost among the rocks
to a door that is closed with a nail.
Seams widen and the paint falls off in curling flakes
from the brave, the bold so little time ago,
the dory high and dry,
anchored in hungry grass.

This is the song of harvest;
the belching trawler raping the sea,
the cobweb ghosts against the window
watching the wilderness uproot the doorsill with a weed.

Fishermen from The Education of Everett Richardson

Silver Donald Cameron

Fishermen are the foundation of a whole reach of the East Coast economy. The fishermen support the boat builders and cordage manufacturers, the dealers in engines and other fishing gear, the machinists and the painters and the cutters in the fish plants, the truckers who drive the refrigerated semi-trailers to Boston and Montreal, the executives in Halifax and Chicago who organize and control the industry. In a town like Canso, *everything* depends on the fishery; fishing is what the town is all about. The schoolteachers, the half-dozen clergy, the shop-keepers, the furnace-oil dealers, the bank clerks, the telephone operator, the fellows in the liquor store, the man who shows the occasional films, even the guys who maintain the wharves and buoys, and the man in the lighthouse on Cranberry Island — there would be precious little call for any of their services without the fishermen; and the big modern fishplant which is the town's chief employer would have to close down. Even Canso's own spectacular government-assisted failure, the Cardinal Protein plant, could never have been proposed without a steady supply of fish offal. Fishing has declined over the years, but it is still an enor-

105

mously important industry, and nowhere more so than in Canso, Petit de Grat, and, to a lesser extent, Mulgrave.

But the importance of fishing is not merely economic. The success of Halifax's own Samuel Cunard in establishing a trans-Atlantic steamship line wiped out the great international trade Nova Scotia boasted in the days of home-built wooden ships; and ever since, the people of the province have gone to sea primarily to catch fish; fishing is nearly all that remains of the province's great seagoing tradition. And yet the sea has made Nova Scotians what they are, to a considerable extent; it has a profound influence on their vision of the world and their sense of human life. Men in little villages building wooden ships and taking them to sea for a living. Men whose competence and courage allow them to survive an environment which in winter seems determined to oblitrate everything alive. Half the people of the province today live and work in Halifax, commuting between the downtown towers and the bedroom suburbs as though they were Torontonians, but they are connected with the villages, they have first cousins and in-laws in Lower Economy or South West Pubnico, and their image of themselves is not bounded by the limits of metropolitan Halifax. "We come from Petit de Grat," said an Acadian girl to me once at a party in the City; but she was born in Halifax and so were her parents. No matter her ancestors probably fled the siege of Louisbourg in 1758 when the French empire was crumbling, and after two centuries they are from Petit de Grat however long they may live in town.

Death by sea looms large in Nova Scotia's vision of life. Gail Fitzpatrick of Mulgrave, who with her fisherman husband Eric was one of the strongest supporters of the strike, lost her father and her only brother at sea. When Everett Richardson and Edison Lumsden fall to gossiping and reminiscing, they identify their friends by the places they were drowned. *You remember old so and so?* No. *He's the one that was drowned off Scatarie Island.* Oh, him! Fishermen's gossip is full of deaths; men swept overboard and left behind by a skipper intent on his fishing; men caught up in nets or winches and crushed or drowned; men trapped in ice-covered ships which became top-heavy and turned turtle. Death by sea is a possibility every working day of a fisherman's life.

The fishermen I know are therefore very direct, very practical, very good at savouring their pleasures. They don't sniff around for information: they ask. *Where d'you come from? What d'you do for a living? What brings you down this way?* They have to know a little biology, a little woodwork and naval architecture, a little mechanics. They see no point in paying someone to do something they can do themselves, and they don't respect people who waste money. Slowly, gradually, Everett Richardson is remodelling his little old house by the highway on the outskirts of Canso. He tears down the ceiling, puts up the panelling, opens up the wall for a new window. He can mend a net, caulk a boat, tear a big marine diesel engine apart and rebuild it.

He drinks enough — or did — that I was once worried that he might become an alcoholic. I was quite wrong. He will quit drinking and "go on the keg" for months at a time. The reason he drank a lot is that he enjoyed it, just as he enjoys sitting on a wharf in the sunlight swapping stories, just as he enjoys taking his family to the beach in the summer, just as he enjoys going out for blueberries and bakeapples in the early fall, just as he enjoys eating the preserves his wife Jean puts up or the big lobsters which sometimes come his way.

People like this are a kind of touchstone of value in Nova Scotian life. They are realists, they cut through pretentiousness like a sharp knife through the belly of a codfish.

Transit West

Peter M. Sanger

Water
Hides seams
A keel
Uncovers.

Birds leave
Unmarked
Their passage
Through air.

Men endure
What they do:
No
Oblivion.

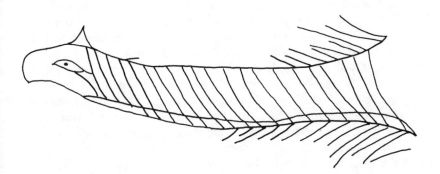

Horned Snake

Rockbound

Frank Parker Day

She was a smart-looking schooner, painted a gleaming black, with a strip of scarlet along her scupper line from stem to stern. Through the clear water, her coppered bottom glimmered, and below her bowsprit was a gilded figurehead that some local artist had carved as a semblance of the young master's little girl, for whom the schooner was named. She had deep, graceful sheer, her spars raked slightly aft, and with a couple of guns mounted bow and stern she might easily have passed for a swift privateer such as sailed those waters a hundred years before her time. With the exception of the *Springwood*, she was the fastest of all the Liscomb fleet. Both her top masts were stepped — something unusual in a banker — her yellow dories were nested on deck, jibs were flapping loose, the peak of the mainsail hoisted to dry, and as the breeze yawed her to and fro on her cable, she seemed to David as buoyant and supple as a gannet riding a wave.

They were soon alongside, and David, at Uriah's order, hastened to put out a rope fender to guard the schooner's new paint from their gunwale. Hand-line Johnny appeared at the rail above them to shout a greeting. He was as smart as his schooner. Although only twenty-five years of age, he was known from Cape Brule to Marmot as a fisherman of great skill and judgment, an accurate navigator and bold sailing master. He dared carry on in half gale, and his reputation for daring, combined with his youth and strength, won for him the admiration and loyalty of his crews. Sailors and fishermen swear by a master who will carry on sail. Nothing warmed Captain Johnny's heart more than to have both topsails bellying and the lee rail under.

David and Martin climbed aboard and carried their dunnage to the banks assigned them in the forecast.

On the same morning the *Sylvia Westner* sailed, and young Martin got his first extended view of the coast, a little part of which he knew so well. He was young Martin in name only, and so called to distinguish him from his uncle in Sanford. Young Martin was not liked on board from the first. He was close-mouthed, greedy at table, and had all the pride and arrogance of the Rockbound Jungs. David, however, upon whom Martin really relied for help and advice, soon became a favourite. His bunk in the forecastle was narrow and cramping for a man of his stature, but that mattered little to him, he was inured to hard beds and by nature a sailor. There were twenty-five men aboard, rigging and paint work were in first-class repair, and the watches light. On the outward voyage he had a two hours' trick at the wheel and the rest of the day to himself.

.   .   .

Hand-line Johnny, with his usual run of good luck, found great schools of cod. He loaded the *Sylvia Westner* with everything he dared carry, and was back in Liscomb from his spring trip in a little more than seven weeks.

Then the *Sylvia Westner* set out on her summer trip, this time to fish the sandy banks to the southward of Sable Island, where shifting channels give grudging passage through the bars. Hand-line Johnny knew the ground well, and it was, of all banks, his favourite. It seemed a marvellous place to David, who could look over the side of his dory into deep green water, see the schools of cod, watch them take the hook or scatter in terror as the dark shadow of shark or albacore hung above them. Near him, the *Sylvia Westner*, her black sides now scarred and scrubbed by chaffing dories, yawed at her cable. The triangular riding sail was set aft, to keep her head to the wind, and around her, in a circle of a mile diameter, her yellow dories danced. Just like an old hen with a flock of yellow chickens, he used to think. When the fish were biting well, he could see captain, cooks, and boys hauling the flashing cod over the vessel's rail. No one idled on Hand-line Johnny's vessel, for he had a passion for loading his schooner quickly, beating all records, and thus proving to the world that hand-lining was a better method of fishing than trawling. To establish this principle, which was, perhaps, of as much value as principles that people accounted more important try to establish, he spared neither himself nor his crew.

On the midday summer sea the *Sylvia Westner*, encircled by her dories and yawing under her riding sail, was a fine sight, but when the long twilight began to fall, softening all lines, she appeared to David romantic and beautiful. Then she was like a pirate ship, with all the excitement and movement of battle. Dories deep to the gunwale bumped alongside, forkfuls of fish flew over the rail, unloaded dories tailed and elbowed astern, the schooner's waist was a welter of slippery cod, splitters flashed their knives by the flare of torches, boys dashed to and fro to fetch and carry, salters sweated in the hold as the split fish came tumbling down the hatchways. A babble of talk and laughter mingled with the smack of fish on the splitting tables and the splash in the washing butts. Hand-line Johnny led the way, and everyone went at top speed. Little wonder he took a crew of picked men!

. . .

That great summer storm which harried Rockbound had its origin in a rotating hurricane that whirled from the Caribbean

Sea to sweep the whole Atlantic coast. It drove past Rockbound and in due time struck the *Sylvia Westner* as she lay riding to the southward of Sable Island. Hand-line Johnny had no wireless to warn him of approaching storms, but for several days he had noted the barometer's fall, and felt in his bones that a great storm was coming. Still, the fishing was good, the vessel almost loaded; given another week, and he would be homeward bound, hold full, and decks kenched high. Five miles to the north lay the *Sadie Oxner*, out of Minden, a trawler, a dangerous rival for his honours, and he vowed to himself to stay on the ground longer than her master dared. At all costs, he must be home earlier and with a bigger fare than the *Springwood*, the *Nova Zembla,* or the *Sadie Oxner*.

So Hand-line Johnny disregarded the strange windless waves, daily increasing in length and height, and with two cables out lay fifteen miles to the southward and in full view of that treacherous crescent of rolling sand dunes, whose horns stretch twenty miles to the westward and fourteen to the eastward, under the green water. At night he saw the two lights, one on the eastern, one on the western end of the giant sand pile, blink warningly at him, and midway between them the dim glow of the life-saving station.

When, in the early part of Saturday evening, the full force of the southeast hurricane suddenly struck the *Sylvia Westner*, her fish-laden dories were alongside, and those empty trailed astern on their long painters. The ninety-mile gale howled through the schooner's spars, and away went scraps and patches of the riding sail torn from spar and boom. The *Sadie Oxner* had long since slipped her cable and departed. Dories had to be got aboard, nested, and lashed, hatch covers fitted and battened down, cables keg-buoyed and cut — there was neither time nor opportunity to get the anchors — foresail lashed down with double stops, and away drove the *Sylvia Westner* under a scrap of double-reefed inner staysail.

Hand-line Johnny and old Caleb Baker, his next-door

113

neighbour on the La Tuque Islands, held the wheel steady, though violent blows of following seas almost tore the spokes from their hands. David, whose trick it was by turn, stood behind them to render assistance if needed. He had no fear in his heart, but gloried in the fury of the gale. It was just like the tempest in his book of verses, rain, wind, thunder, and a lee shore. Would Captain Johnny, he wondered, try to bring her into the wind when close to the bar, or would he wear ship and try the other tack? Either plan would be hazardous. The wind tore the sou'wester from his head and whirled it through the flying spume of the sea. Holding fast to the main sheet, he stood bareheaded and smiling; this was the stuff to drive from his mind thoughts of hopeless love.

Captain Johnny, as he steadied the wheel, knew that it was impossible to haul the *Sylvia Westner* up in the wind and heave her to; that meant setting the peak of the mainsail, and that could not be considered in this roaring gale. To put her even for a moment in the trough of that mountainous sea might trip her, and even if the manoeuvre were successful and he hove her to, she would eventually drift ashore. No, the only chance was to drive straight on before the gale. Darkness had come, but the weather was clear, and he could see the blink of the eastern light on his port bow. If he held his course he would run over the middle of the eastern bar. The tide was at the top of the flood, there were deep channels through the sand, perhaps God would guide him to one; in moderate weather, he had run over the bar many times before. As he dared not bring his vessel to the wind, he could only make out as far as possible to the bar's end without putting her in the trough of the sea. The double-reefed staysail cracked, bellied, and tugged desperately at sheet and halliard; if that went he must manage somehow to set a corner of a jib.

Four men of the watch, young Martin among them, were on the forward deck, lashed to stanchion or belaying pin, for the seas swept her from stern to stem. As Martin clung fast to his lashing, he bitterly resented the fact that his father had sent him from his island home. Fishing from Rockbound was by comparison safe; there was nothing like having solid ground beneath your feet at night. Another time he would resist the old man. He drove some fear from his mind by reckoning up his share when the *Sylvia Westner* sold her fish in Liscomb. All the other men of the crew were below in forecastle or afterhouse, companionway and forecastle hatch closed tight; they could do no good on deck and had boundless faith in the luck and skill of their "old man" Hand-line Johnny.

Now the seas began to break short with a peculiar ragged whiteness. "We're in shoal water near de bar," yelled Hand-line Johnny to old Caleb Baker. "God give us luck dis night." Wind furies shrieked, stays and halliards groaned with the straining spars, piled dories tugged at their lashings, a water butt broke loose and went booming along the deck to crash into the forecastle hatch. A mountain of white water gathered behind the *Sylvia Westner*, rose with slow, malicious dignity, and crashed down upon her poop. David clung with arms and legs to the main sheet, but both steersmen were dashed against the deckhouse. Captain Johnny's right hand held fast the wheel spoke, but when the sea washed clear and he staggered to his feet old Caleb Baker was gone. At a sign from the young master David stepped forward and took his place.

At that moment the *Sylvia Westner* struck; Hand-line Johnny had no luck that night. All was over in the twinkling of an eye. The vessel, deep-laden, was travelling at the rate of twenty knots, and a tooth of black bottom rock whipped bottom and keelson from her as cleanly as a boy with a sharp jackknife slits a shaving from a pine stick. Two thousand quintals of split fish and the unwetted salt dropped down upon the yellow sands; out came the spars with a rending crash, and deck and upper hull turned over. Within ten seconds of her striking, every man of the crew was in the sea. Away they went, young Martin still lashed to a bit of bulwark among them, poor scraps of humanity, weighed down with soaked clothing and long boots; a flash of yellow oilskins, hoarse cries that made no sound in the fierce tumult, and they were gone. Some swam a stroke or two, some clung for an instant to trailing rigging or broken dory, but few clung long in that mad breaking sea.

David, as the sea engulfed him, caught the trailing end of a dory's painter, whipped it twice around his body beneath the armpits, and tied it fast with a double net hitch. Then, as a sea drove the dory near him, he wormed his great right hand through the loop, at the dory's stem, and let himself hang limply by the wrist. He kicked off his rubber boots, tore loose the shoulder straps of his oil pants, and wriggled his legs free. He gasped for breath when his face was clear; he was bewildered but not afraid. This was the Tempest without the saving magic. A pleasant numbness beginning at his feet stole over him.

·　　·　　·

The roaring southeaster drove the dory, to which David was lashed, shoreward. Life guards, who had seen the last flicker of the *Sylvia Westner's* lights, patrolled the beaches through the night, and one caught a glimpse of yellow dory in the white water. Wading into the surf waist deep, they dragged it ashore. To their astonishment a man was fast to the painter, his right hand, black and cruelly swollen, wedged in the dory's loop. They cut the ropes clear, carried him beyond the reach of breakers that yelled for their prey, and laid him in the lee of a steep sand dune. There they built a fire of driftwood, cut his soaked clothing from him, and wrapped him in warm wool blankets. His right arm, broken above the elbow by the barging of the sodden dory in the surf, hung limp and distorted. He seemed dead as a stone. Still, as there was some warmth in his body, they prized open his clenched teeth and poured brandy in his mouth. They pulled his tongue forward, jerked the sea water from him, and by relays inflated and deflated his lungs by a mechanical process. Yes, there was a flicker of life in him. They

116

strove to restore him with all their vigour, so careful are men of life nigh lost, so careless of it in full flush. When breathing was restored they carried him on a stretcher to the life-saving station and laid him in a warm bed.

The name on the dory told them the name of the vessel lost, but there was nothing in David's clothing to identify him save a sea-soaked book on the flyleaf of which appeared the name Dauphiny. "One o' dem Dauphinys down La Tuque way," they conjectured, and sent word to the main that the *Sylvia Westner* had been lost, and a man named Dauphiny washed ashore, living. It was only at the end of two days that David was able to whisper: "I'se David Jung from Rockbound."

Biography

Charles Bruce

His speckled pastures dipped to meet the beach
Where the old fish huts stood. At his front door
A man could stand and see the whole wide reach
Of blue Atlantic. But he stayed ashore.

He stayed ashore and plowed, and drilled his rows,
And planned his hours and finished what he planned.
And made his profits: colts and calves and ewes
And buildings and piled stone and harrowed land.

He was a careful man, a trifle cold
To meet and talk to. There were some who thought
His hand was a bit grasping, when he sold;
A little slow to open when he bought.

But no one said it that way. When you heard
His habits mentioned, there would be a pause.
And then the soft explanatory word.
They said he was dry-footed. And he was.

If the sea infixes
some nameless and
unslakable yearning
in a man's eyes,
the farm yokes
the facts of memory
to his every breath.
And more than the
fisherman with his
single-hearted gaze,
he comes to be the
sum, substance,
and museum of
its thronging
assembly.

The Mosherville Road

Alden Nowlan

If a man wishes to be sure
of the road he treads on, he
must close his eyes and walk
in the dark.

St. John of the Cross

It is nowhere so dark
   as in the country
      where I was born.
I remember nights
   I held my hand
      an inch from my eyes
and saw nothing.
   Yet I kept putting one
      foot in front of the other
and don't recall ever falling
   into the ditch,
      though I was so aware
of it, three feet deep,
   on both sides of me
      with gravel walls
and filthy water
   at the bottom of it,
      that it seems to me now
I must have gone into it,
   at least once
      and forgotten. There was glass
from broken bottles
   and everything else
      that gets thrown from cars
in that ditch and thorn bushes grew
   on the opposite side of it,
      and there were trees

and night birds
   and flying insects
      I couldn't see.
Usually I talked
   to myself and sometimes I sang
      as I stumbled along
and it wasn't until tonight
   almost twenty years
      later I began to realize
how much I was afraid.

Paid-Up Member

Will R. Bird

It was raining a little at noon but Simon Lasher drove out to his corner lot with the disk harrow. He had seen Dickie go up the back road and he meant to intercept him as he returned; he had cleaned and oiled his old army rifle, and he meant to use it.

Simon gritted his teeth as he drove. Jim Dickie had asked for trouble. He had come into the settlement and bought the farm that Simon was on the point of buying. True, he and Hank Wheeler had disagreed on the price, but what right had an outsider to come in and pay more than the land was worth? Then, insult added to injury, Dickie had taken Simon's girl from him. It was carrying things too far.

Simon hurried his horses. He must get to the road corner a few minutes before Dickie came in sight. He held the rifle and a shovel between his knees, and he swung his whip sharply. Folks said Simon never drove without a whip, but how could one hurry horses without it? And where would he be if he had not hurried? In ten years he had paid for his farm, and now had his house in readiness for a bride.

At the corner of the field he stopped his horses. The ground dipped slightly, forming a small hollow, and he dug in the centre of it, scooping a short, shallow trench. He had not got it as deep as he wished when he saw his horses prick up their ears. Some-

one was coming. He dropped his shovel. Jim Dickie was plod-
ding past, his head down to the fine rain. Simon sneered. No one
but Dickie would go in a rain to Hank Wheeler's post office.

"He comes regular," Hank had reported. "He gets soldier
magazines and Legion papers. He's a paid-up member if he does
live out here."

"Paid-up member!" Simon had jeered. "What good's that
to him? Will it help him farm?"

He pretended to be tinkering with the disk harrow. The rifle
was on the ground behind the disks.

"Hi," he called. "Been for mail? Come over. I want to show
you something."

Dickie turned, his pale face friendly. "Yes, I got something
I been expecting, something special for returned men ..."

"Come and see where I've been diggin'," interrupted
Simon.

He hated soldier stuff as he hated this man who had won
Mary Hawkins from him, and the solemn way in which Dickie
could recite "In Flanders Fields". Such rot!

Mary and he had quarrelled when he criticized the poem,
and Mary had refused him her company. And now, a friend had
told Simon in the morning, she and Dickie were to be married as
soon as the school term ended. So Simon had cleaned his rifle.

Dickie carefully fished an envelope from his wet jacket as
he came to where Simon had dug. "See what the Legion sent
me," he said proudly, holding it out. "It's ..."

Crack! The sullen report of a rifle. Simon had looped the
reins about his wrist before he fired, and for a moment he was
busy jerking the horses to a standstill, then he swung them
around to where the limp body was pitched, face down, half into
the cavity. His aim had been true. A dreadful redness was well-
ing from the collar of Dickie's shirt. "Blast you!" grated Simon.
"You kin be a paid-up member of that hole till Kingdom
Come."

The horses quieted and Simon caught up the shovel. He had

heard the chug-chug of a wheezy motor in the distance. It was Hank Wheeler's car. A twist of his heel buried the envelope Dickie had dropped, a single push straightened the body in the trench. He flung the rifle in beside the dead man and shovelled hurriedly. When the old flivver came in sight Simon was seated on his harrow and had just crossed the spaded earth. Twenty minutes later no one could have found the spot where he had dug.

At six o'clock Wheeler knocked at Simon's door. He was county sheriff as well as postmaster. "Did you see Jim Dickie this afternoon?" he asked bluntly.

"Yes, I did,' said Simon. "He passed when I was harrowing". Why?"

"He ain't been seen since," said Hank, as bluntly as before.

"That's strange." Simon simulated surprise. "Maybe he's at one of the neighbours."

"I been all around," said Hank. "You don't know anything, eh?"

"Me? No, I don't," said Simon smoothly, "I'll send you word if I see him."

Three months had passed since Jim Dickie vanished. Simon went to his hoeing contentedly. Mary was recovering from the shock, had got her colour back. He would go and call on her in a few days.

He pulled weeds with a vim. Everything had gone better than he expected. There hadn't been much fuss over Dickie's disappearance, not as much as he had dreaded. And Dickie's Legion had been a joke. An official had come one day and talked with Hank, that was all that had been done. Paid-up member — pooh!

Hank had never seemed the same but perhaps the sheriff's complete failure to find a clue to Dickie's murderer accounted for that. Simon had often looked at the corner lot, now a shimmering green, inches deep. Who would guess its secret? It was good ground and the grain was doing fine. In the fall he would scoop more earth in the hollow at the corner, fill it in.

When he reached the house at supper-time Hank Wheeler and an officer from the city met him. Handcuffs were snapped on Simon's wrist before he could take in what had been said. Hank enlightened him.

"What — me — arrested for murderin' Dickie?" shouted Simon. "You're crazy. I don't know nothin' about him."

"No?" Hank's voice sent shivers up Simon's spine. "You'll have a hard time makin' the judge believe that. You harrowed that field the day Jim was killed — and it was your rifle we found beside him."

"You — you — found —" Simon's face whitened, became ghastly. He seemed to wilt.

"We did," said Hank grimly. "All I been doin' was watch that field of yours. I knowed they'd sprout if they was near the surface."

Simon licked his dry lips. "What — sprouted?" he whispered.

"Poppies," snapped Wheeler as they led Simon to his car. "Poor Jim got an envelope full of seed that day — a special good kind the Legion sent to paid-up members."

The Rebellion
of Young David

Ernest Buckler

There are times when you can only look at your son and say his
name over and over in your mind.

I would say, "David, David . . ." nights when he was asleep
— the involuntary way you pass your hand across your eyes
when your head aches, though there is no way for your hand to
get inside. It seemed as if it must all have been my fault.

I suppose any seven-year-old has a look of accusing innocence when he is asleep, an assaulting grudgelessness. But it
seemed to me that he had it especially. It seemed incredible that
when I'd told him to undress he'd said, "You make me!" his
eyes dark and stormy. It seemed incredible that those same legs
and hands, absolutely pliant now, would ever be party to that
isolating violence of his again.

His visible flesh was still; yet he was always moving in a
dream. Maybe he'd cry, "Wait . . . Wait up, Art." Where was I
going in the dream, what was I doing, that even as I held him in
my arms he was falling behind?

He called me "Art," not "Dad." The idea was: we were
pals.

I had never whipped him. The thought of my wife — who

126

died when David was born — had something to do with that, I guess. And a curious suggestion of vulnerability about his wire-thin body, his perceptive face, so contrasted with its actual belligerence that the thought of laying a hand on him — well, I just couldn't do it. We were supposed to *reason* things out.

Sometimes that worked. Sometimes it didn't.

He *could* reason, as well as I. His body would seem to vibrate with obedience. His friendship would be absolutely unwithholding. "You stepped on my hand," he'd say, laughing, though his face pinched with the pain of it, "but that doesn't matter, does it, Art? Sometimes you can't see people's hands when they stick them in the way." Or if we were fishing, he'd say, "You tell me when to pull on the line, won't you, Art... just right *when*."

Then, without any warning whatever, he'd become possessed by this automatic inaccessible mutiny.

I'd get the awful feeling then that we were both lost. That whatever I'd done wrong had not only failed, but that he'd never know I'd been *trying* to do it right for him. Worse still, that his mind was rocked by some blind contradiction he'd never understand himself.

Maybe I'd be helping him with a reading lesson. I tried to make a game of it, totalling the words he named right against words he named wrong. He'd look at me, squinting up his face into a contortion of deliberate ingratiation. He'd say, "Seventeen right and only one wrong... wouldn't that make you *laugh*, Art?" then maybe the very next word I'd ask him, he'd slump against the table in a pretended indolence; or flop the book shut while the smile was still on my face.

Or maybe we'd be playing with his new baseball bat and catcher's mitt.

His hands were too small to grasp the bat properly and his fingers were lost in the mitt. But he couldn't have seemed more obliteratingly happy when he did connect with the ball. ("Boy, that was a solid hit, wasn't it, Art? You throw them to me *just* right, Art, just *right*") He'd improvise rules of his own for the game. His face would twist with the delight of communicating them to me.

Then, suddenly, when he'd throw the ball, he'd throw it so hard that the physical smart of it on my bare fingers would sting me to exasperation.

"All right," I'd say coolly, "if you don't want to play, I'll go hoe the garden."

I'd go over to the garden, watching him out of the corner of my eye. He'd wander forlornly about the yard. Then I'd see him coming slowly toward the garden (where his tracks still showed along the top of the row of carrots he'd raced through yesterday). He'd come up behind me and say, "I have to walk right between the rows, don't I? Gardens are hard *work*, aren't they, Art... you don't want anyone stepping on the rows."

David, David....

The strange part, it wasn't that discipline had no effect because it made no impression.

One evening he said out of a blue sky. "*You're* so smart, Art ... I haven't got a brain in my head, not one. You've got so many *brains*, Art, *brains*...." I was completely puzzled.

Then I remembered: I had countered with complete silence when he'd called me "dumb" that morning. I'd forgotten the incident entirely. But he hadn't. Though he'd been less rather than more tractable since then, he'd been carrying the snub around with him all day.

Or take the afternoon there was only one nickel in his small black purse. I saw him take it out and put it back several times before he came and asked me for another. He never asked me for money unless he wanted it terribly. I gave him another nickel. He went to the store and came back with two Cokes. For some reason he had to treat me.

My face must have shown my gratification. He said, with his devastating candour, "You look happier with me than you did this morning, don't you, Art?"

I couldn't even recall the offence that time. *He* had felt my displeasure, though on my part it must have been quite unconscious.

What had I done wrong? I didn't know.

Unless it was that, when he was small, I'd kept a harness on him in the yard. He rebelled, instinctively, at any kind of bond. But what else could I do? Our house was on a blind corner. What else could I do, when I had the picture of the strength of his slight headlong body falling against the impersonal strength of a truck or the depth of a well?

David, David....

I said,"David, David..." out loud, that particular afternoon he lay so still on the ground; because this is the way it had happened.

I had taken him fencing with me that morning. It was one of those perfect spring mornings when even the woods seem to breath but a clean water-smell. He was very excited. He'd never been to the back of the pasture before.

I carried the axe and the mall. He carried the staple-box and the two hammers. Sometimes he walked beside me, sometimes ahead.

There was something about him that always affected me when I watched him moving *back to*. I'd made him wear his rubber boots because there was a swamp to cross. Now the sun was getting hot. I wished I'd let him wear his sneakers and carried him across the swamp. There was something about the heavy boots *not* slowing up his eager movement and the thought that they must be tiring him without his consciousness of it.

I asked him if his legs weren't tired. "Noooooo," he scoffed. As if that were the kind of absurd question people kid each other with to clinch the absolute perfection of the day. Then he added, "If your legs do get a little tired when you're going some place, that doesn't hurt, does it, Art?"

His unpredictable twist of comment made him good company, in an adult way. Yet there was no unnatural shadow of precocity about him. His face had a kind of feature-smalling brightness that gave him a peaked look when he was tired or disappointed, and when his face was washed and the water on his hair, for town, a kind of shining. But it was as childlike and unwithholding as the clasp of his hand. (Or maybe he didn't look much different from any other child. Maybe I couldn't see him straight because I loved him.)

This was one of his days of intense, jubilant, communicativeness. One of his "How come?" days. As if by his questions and my answers we (and we alone) could find out about everything.

If I said anything mildly funny he worked himself up into quite a glee. I knew his laughter was a little louder than natural. His face would twitch a little, renewing it, each time I glanced at him. But that didn't mean that his amusement was false. I knew that his intense willingness to think anything funny I said was as funny as anything could possibly be, tickled him more than the joke itself. "You always say such funny things, Art!"

We came to the place where I had buried the horse. Dogs had dug away the earth. The brackets of its ribs and the chalky grimace of its jaws stared whitely in the bright sun.

He looked at it with sudden quietness beyond mere attention; as if something invisible were threatening to come too close. I thought he was a little pale. He had never seen a skeleton before.

"Those bones can't move, *can* they, Art?" he said.

"No," I said.

"How can bones move?"

"Oh, they have to have flesh on them, and muscles, and...."

"Well, could he move when he was just dead? I mean right then, when he was right just dead?"

"No."

"How come?"

I was searching for a reply when he moved very close to me.

"Could you carry the hammers, Art, please?" he said.

I put the hammers in my back overalls pocket.

"Could *you* carry an axe and a mall both in one hand?" he said.

I took the axe in my left hand, with the mall, so that now we each had a hand free. He took my hand and tugged me along the road.

He was quiet for a few minutes, then he said, "Art? What goes away out of your muscles when you're dead?"

He was a good boy all morning. He was really a help. If you fence alone you can't carry all the tools through the brush at once. You have to replace a stretch of rotted posts with the axe and mall; then return to where you've left the staple-box and hammers and go over the same ground again, tightening the wire.

He carried the staple-box and hammers and we could complete the operation as we went. He held the wire taut while I drove the staples. He'd get his voice down very low. "The way you do it, Art, see, you get the claw of your hammer right behind a barb so it won't slip . . . so it won't *slip*, Art, see?" As if he'd discovered some trick that would now be a conspiratorial secret between just us two. The obbligato of manual labour was like a quiet stitching together of our presences.

We started at the far end of the pasture and worked toward home. It was five minutes past eleven when we came within sight of the skeleton again. The spot where my section of the fence ended. That was fine. We could finish the job before noon and not have to walk all the way back again after dinner. It was aggravating when I struck three rotten posts in a row; but we could still finish, if we hurried. I though David looked a little pale again.

"You take off those heavy boots and rest, while I go down to the intervale and cut some posts," I said. There were no trees growing near the fence.

"All right, Art." He was very quiet. There was that look of suspension in his flesh he'd get sometimes when his mind was working on something it couldn't quite manoeuvre.

It took me no more than twenty minutes to cut the posts, but when I carried them back to the fence he wasn't there.

"Bring the staples, chum," I shouted. He didn't pop out from behind any bush.

"David! David!" I called, louder. There was only that hollow stillness of the wind rustling the leaves when you call to someone in the woods and there is no answer. He had completely disappeared.

I felt a sudden irritation. Of all the damn times to beat it home without telling me!

I started to stretch the wire alone. But an uneasiness began to insinuate itself. Anyone could follow that wide road home. But what if... I didn't know just what... but what if something ...? Oh dammit, I'd have to go find him.

I kept calling him all the way along the road. There was no answer. How could he get out of sound so quickly, unless he ran? He must have run all the way. But why? I began to run, myself.

My first reaction when I saw him standing by the house, looking toward the pasture, was intense relief. Then, suddenly my irritation was compounded.

He seemed to sense my annoyance, even from a distance. He began to wave, as if in propitiation. He had a funny way of waving, holding his arm out still and moving his hand up and down very slowly. I didn't wave back. When I came close enough that he could see my face he stopped waving.

"I thought you'd come home without me, Art," he said.

"Why should you think that?" I said, very calmly.

He wasn't defiant as I'd expected him to be. He looked as if he were relieved to see me; but as if at the sight of me coming from that direction he knew he'd done something wrong. Now

132

he was trying to pass the thing off as an amusing quirk in the way things had turned out. Though half-suspecting that this wouldn't go over. His tentative over-smiling brushed at my irritation, but didn't dislodge it.

"I called to you, Art," he said.

I just looked at him, as much as to say, do you think I'm deaf?

"Yes, I called. I thought you'd come home some other way."

"Now I've got to traipse all the way back there this afternoon to finish one rod of fence," I said.

"I thought you'd gone and left me," he said.

I ignored him, and walked past him into the house.

He didn't eat much dinner, but he wasn't defiant about that, either, as he was, sometimes, when he refused to eat. And after dinner he went out and sat down on the banking, by himself. He didn't know that his hair was sticking up through the heart-shaped holes in the skullcap with all the buttons pinned on it.

When it was time to go back to the woods again he hung around me with his new bat and ball. Tossing the ball up himself and trying to hit out flies.

"Boy, you picked out the very best bat there was, didn't you, Art?" he said. I knew he thought I'd toss him a few. I didn't pay any attention to what he was doing.

When I started across the yard, he said, "Do you want me to carry the axe this afternoon? That makes it *easier* for you, doesn't it, Art?"

"I'll be back in an hour or so," I said. "You play with Max."

He went as far as the gate with me. Then he stopped. I didn't turn around. It sounds foolish, but everything between us was on such an adult basis that it wasn't until I bent over to crawl through the barbed wire fence that I stole a glance at him, covertly. He was tossing the ball up again and trying to hit it. It always fell to the ground, because the bat was so unwieldy and because he had one eye on me.

I noticed he still had on his hot rubber boots. I had intended to change them for his sneakers. He was the sort of child who seems unconsciously to invest his clothes with his own mood. The thought of his clothes, when he was forlorn, struck me as hard as the thought of his face.

Do you know the kind of thoughts you have when you go back alone to a job which you have been working at happily with another? When that work together has ended in a quarrel ... with your accusations unprotested, and, after that, your rejection of his overtures unprotested too?

I picked up my tools and began to work. But I couldn't seem to work quickly.

I'd catch myself, with the hammer slack in my hands, thinking about crazy things like his secret pride in the new tie (which he left outside his pullover until he saw that the other children had theirs inside) singling him so abatedly from the town children, the Saturday I took him to the matinee, that I felt an unreasonable rash of protectiveness toward him.. . . Of him laughing dutifully at the violence in the comedy, but crouching a little toward me, while the other children, who were not nearly so violent as he, shrieked together in a seizure of delight.

I thought of his scribblers, with the fixity there of the letters which his small hand had formed earnestly, but awry.

I thought of those times when the freak would come upon him to recount all his trangressions of the day, insisting on his guilt with phrases of my own I had never expected him to remember.

I thought of him playing ball with the other children.

At first they'd go along with the outlandish variations he'd introduce into the game, because it was his equipment. Then, somehow, *they'd* be playing with the bat and glove and he'd be out of it, watching.

I thought now of him standing there, saying, "Boy, I hope

my friends come to play with me early tomorrow, *early*, Art"—though I knew that if they came at all their first question would be, "Can we use your bat and glove?"

I thought of him asleep. I thought, if anything should ever happen to him that's the way he would look.

I laughed; to kid myself for being such a soft and sentimental fool. But it was no use. The feeling came over me, immediate as the sound of a voice, that something *was* happening to him right now.

It was coincidence, of course, but I don't believe that ... because I had started to run even before I came over the crest of the knoll by the barn. Before I saw the cluster of excited children by the horse stable.

I couldn't see David among them, but I saw the ladder against the roof, I saw Max running toward the stable, with my neighbour running behind him. I knew, by the way the children looked at me—with that half-discomfited awe that was always in their faces whenever any recklessness of David's was involved—what had happened.

"He fell off the roof," one of them said.

I held him, and I said, "David, David...."

He stirred. "Wait," he said drowsily, "Wait up, Art...."

I suppose it's foolish to think that if I hadn't been right there, right then, to call his name, he would never have come back. Because he was only stunned. The doctor could scarcely find a bruise on him. (I don't know just why my eyes stung when the doctor patted his head in admiration of his patience, when the exhaustive examination was over. He was always so darned quiet and brave at the doctor's and dentist's.)

I read to him the rest of the afternoon. He'd sit quiet all day, with the erasure on his face as smooth as the erasure of sleep, if you read to him.

After supper, I decided to finish the fence. It was the season of long days.

"Do you want to help me finish the fence?" I said. I thought he'd be delighted.

"No," he said. "You go on. I'll wait right here. Right here, Art."

"Who's going to help me stretch the wire?" I said.

"All right," he said.

He scarcely spoke until we got almost back to the spot where the skeleton was. Then he stopped and said, "We better go back, Art. It's going to be dark."

"G'way with ya," I said. "It won't be dark for hours." It wouldn't be although the light *was* an eerie after-supper light.

"I'm going home," he said. His voice and his face were suddenly defiant.

"You're not going home," I said sharply. "Now come on, hurry up."

I was carrying an extra pound of staples I had picked up in town that afternoon. He snatched the package from my hand. Before I could stop him he broke the string and strewed them far and wide.

I suppose I was keyed up after the day, for I did then what I had never done before. I took him and held him and I put it into him, hard and thoroughly.

He didn't try to escape. For the first few seconds he didn't make a sound. The only reaction of his defiance was a kind of crouching in his eyes when he first realized what I was going to do. Then he began to cry. He cried and cried.

"You're *going* home," I said, "and you're going right to *bed*."

I could see the marks of my fingers on his bare legs, when I undressed him. He went to sleep almost immediately. But though it was perfectly quiet downstairs for reading, the words of my book might have been any others.

When I got him up to the toilet, he had something to say, as

136

usual. But this time he was wide awake. I sat down on the side of his bed for a minute.

"Bones make you feel funny, don't they, Art?" was what he said.

I remembered then.

I remembered that the skeleton was opposite the place where he sat down to rest. I remembered how he had shrunk from it on the way back. I remembered then that the wind had been blowing *away* from me, when I was cutting the posts. That's why I hadn't heard him call. I thought of him calling, and then running along the road alone, in the heavy, hot, rubber boots.

David, David, I thought, do I always fail you like that? . . . the awful misinterpretation a child has to endure! I couldn't answer him.

"I thought you'd gone home, Art," he said.

"I'm sorry," I said. I couldn't seem to find any words to go on with.

"I'm sorry too I threw the staples," he said eagerly.

"I'm sorry I spanked you."

"No, no," he said. "You spank me every time I do that, won't you, Dad? . . . *spank* me, Dad."

His night-face seemed happier than I had ever seen it. As if the trigger-spring of his driving restlessness had been finally cut.

I won't say it came in a flash. It wasn't such a simple thing as that. But could that be what I had done wrong?

He called me "Dad." Could it be that a child would rather have a father than a pal? ("Wait. . . . Wait up, Art.") By spanking him I had abrogated the adult partnership between us and set him free. He could cry. His guilt could be paid for all at once and absolved.

It wasn't the spanking that had been cruel. What had been cruel were all the times I had snubbed him as you might an adult—with implication of shame. There was no way he could get over that. The unexpiable residue of blame piled up in him. Shutting him out, spreading (who can tell what unlikely symptoms a child's mind will translate it into?), blocking his access to me, to other children, even to himself. His reaction was violence, deviation. Any guilt a sensitive child can't be absolved of at once he blindly adds to, whenever he thinks of it, in a kind of desperation.

I had worried about failing him. That hadn't bothered him. What had bothered him was an adult shame I had taught him, I saw now, for failing *me*.

I kissed him good-night. "Okay, son," I said, "I'll spank you sometimes."

He nodded, smiling. "Dad," he said then, "how come you knew I jumped off the roof?"

That should have brought me up short—how much farther apart we must be than I'd imagined if he was driven to jump off a roof to shock me back into contact. "Jumped," he said, not "fell."

But somehow it didn't. It gave me the most liberating kind of hope. Because it hadn't been a question, really. It had been a statement. "How come you *knew* . . .?" He hadn't the slightest doubt that no matter what he did, wherever I was I would know it, and that wherever I was I would come.

Anyhow, it is a fine day today, and we have just finished the fence. He is playing ball with the other children as I put this down. Their way.

The First Born Son

Ernest Buckler

The pale cast of fatigue smudged Martin's skin and little grooves of it emptied into the corners of his mouth. But this land was his own, and a son of his own flesh was holding the plow that broke it. His thoughts were tired half-thoughts but they did not ache.

He felt the wine of the fall day and for a minute his feet wandered, inattentive, from the furrow. The dogged, slow-eyed oxen followed him, straining nose-down at his heels. The plow ran out wide in the sod. David tried to flip over the furrow with a sudden wrench of the handles, but the chocolate-curling lip of earth broke and the share came clear.

"Whoa!" David yelled.

"Whoa!" Martin roared at the oxen.

"For God's sake, Dad, can't you watch where you're going? It's hard enough to hold this damn thing when you keep 'em straight."

"Now don't get high," Martin said. But there was no echo of David's temper in his voice. He knew David was tired. And David could not learn to handle his weariness. He fought it. It was no use to do that. If you let it come and go, quietly, after supper it made a lazy song in your muscles and was good to think about. Martin remembered the night David was born. They had thought Ellen would die. It was Christmas Eve. There

139

was not a breath of wind in the moonlit, Christmas-kindled air. Snow lay in kind folds on the ground, shadowed in the dead-still moonlight like the wrinkles of a white cloak. On the brook Martin could watch the gay, meaningless movements of the children skating. And sometimes a fragment of their heartless laughter would break away and fall inside the room. Ellen's pain-tight face stared at her pale hands outside the quilt. The kind-smelling Christmas tree was a cruel mockery. Now and then Martin would go outside and listen, bare-headed, for the doctor's sleigh-bells, trying to separate their faint, far-off tinkle from the frost-crackle of the spruces. He would think he heard them. Then there would be nothing. Runner tracks shone like isinglass in the moonlight. He heard nothing but the heartless laughter of the children.

It seemed hours later, when he was not listening at all, that he looked out and all at once the dark body of the horse turned in the gate, by the corner of the house. His heart gave a great leap. The helplessness left him. This man could hold Ellen back from death. The moonlight seemed to turn warm. After the doctor went in with Ellen the laughing of the children did not seem so far-off and strange.

The quick white grip of fear came again when he heard the doctor's hand on the door again ... but Martin looked up and the doctor was *smiling*. Suddenly the whole night was a great, neighbourly, tear-starting friend. He had a son now. He knew it would be a son.

Martin felt shy to kiss Ellen in front of the doctor, but there was a new peace and a strange swagger in his soul. When he got the doctor's horse for him, it seemed like the best horse in all the world; and half-ashamed and half-afraid not to, but somehow wanting desperately to thank *someone*, he knelt down for a minute on the hay and prayed. Outside the barn, the voices of the children laughing were a glad song in his ears, now. In the bedroom, Ellen murmured "My own little Jesus" ... and the thick spruce-cosy smell of the Christmas tree and the shining moon-

140

light outside and the soft peace after danger past clothed the minutes in a sweet armour ... A son ... A son ... And Ellen well ... Martin couldn't believe how good it was. He would never die now. He had a son, now ... when he was too old to break up the land he loved, any more, this son would come in at night and they would plan together, just the same. This son's sons ...

"Well, maybe you think it's *easy* to hold this damn thing," David said. It *must* be that he's tired, Martin thought. He can't mean that ... this same David ... my own son cannot find it hard to plow this land of our own. I never found it so, when I was young. Plowed land was always the prettiest sight in the world to me. It was always good at the end of the day, to stand and look over the brown waves of earth and know that I had opened my land to the sun and the air and the rain. I don't like to hear this son of mine talk that way. He says too many things like that. I don't like to hear my son talk that way. The plowed land was here before us and it will last after us and our hands should be proud to work in it.

"Haw," Martin called, and the lip of the earth curled back and buried the grass again.

In the city, David thought, their bodies are not dead-tired now. They have not walked all day in their own tracks ... back and forth, back and forth, in their own damn tracks. There is movement and lights and laughing. Every day there is something *new* ... something to keep alive for. The same people here ... the same talk ... the same eternal drudgery ... your nose in the ground all day long, from morning till night, like a damned ox ... cooped up in that damned circle of trees.

The last brown beech leaves on the hardwood hill drifted down to the ground, dreamily, a little sad to die. A flock of partridges made their heavy headlong flight into an apple tree and began to bud. In the fields, the potato stalks lay in blackened heaps. The earth was grey and brown. All the colour was in the sky or hung in the thin air. Only the stray pumpkins, left to ripen on the withered vines, gave back any of it. They were like bubbles of the sad October sunshine. Martin loved these quick chill dusks, and then later the kind eye of lamplight in the window, and the friendly, wood-warmed, table-set kitchen.

They came to the end of the furrow. Martin split the rest of the acre with his eye.

"Will we finish her before supper, son?" he asked.

"Do you want to work all night too!"

Martin stopped the oxen.

"What's wrong with you today, Dave?" he said. "If you planned to go after the partridges..."

"Partridges, hell!"

"Well then, what's..."

David hesitated.

"I'm so damn sick of this place I..."

"Is *that* so!" Martin said slowly. "What's wrong with this place?" He kicked over a sod with the toe of his shabby boot. An old man looked out of his face for the first time. It was true, then ... It had never been because David was tired or lonely or weak or young... It was because David had always *hated* this land... the land that would be his own some day. A sick little cloud settled on his heart. He *had* no son, then.

"What's *wrong* with it?" David said. "The same damn thing over and over from morning till night ... every day and every day ... what future is there for anyone here?" David kept his back bent to the plow handles. He felt a little mean and ashamed when he heard the sound of his own words.

"What future is there here?" The question sounded meaningless to Martin. He had the truth, to contradict it. There is the first day in April when the fields stir again and it is good all day just to feel your breathing ... There is the sky-blue August day when the whole green wind is full of leaves and growing, and Sunday morning you walk in the waving growth-full garden rows and wish you could keep this day forever, hold it back from going ... It is good, too, when the snow whistles cold and mournful because it can never get inside the pane to warm itself

142

... It is *all* good, all of it ... Men live here as long as their sons live, to see the clearings their axes have made and the living grass that sprang from their tracks in the first furrow and the green things their hands gave life to ... "The same thing over and over..." Martin did not speak. Only his sick thoughts pleaded, patiently, silently, incredulously. We did not plow yesterday, David. We took the day off and last night this time we sat at the edge of the woods and waited for the shy-eyed deer to come out into the old back field.

I thought it was good to sit there and smoke with my son after we boiled the supper kettle, not talking much but not feeling the silence either, and watch the dead leaves drifting down past the rocks in the cool-talking brook. The fire itself felt good, in spite of the sun, and it was good to hear the nervous twitter of the partridges in the apple trees just before it got too dark to pick out their heads along the sights of the gun ... Or is this like the day last spring we nodded at each other across the pool with the foam on it each time we held a broken-neck trout throbbing in the tight of our palms? Or the day we cursed the heat in the alder-circled meadow and our shirts stuck to our backs like broken blisters? The hay smelt good that night, just the same, and it was good to hear the wagon wheels groan on the sill just before the dark thunder-frown of the sky burst and the barn roof beat back the rain. I remember the night we ate our first supper in the house I had built with my own hands. That night the neighbours came in, and we danced half the night to the fiddles. It was easy with everyone, like with brothers, and we loved them all ... and it was good that night to lie in bed and let sleep's drowsy wind blow out the candles of thought. The day they brought your brother Peter home loose in their arms before it was dinner time, his dead body so broken your mother could not hold it, that day was different... And the next day... And the next day...

"Well, what kind of a place suits *you?*" Martin said at last. David straightened.

143

"The city, of course! Who'd want to live in this God-for-saken hole when you can get a job in the city?"

"Did you say the *city?*"

"Yeah. The city," he said laconically.

Martin listened with sick wonder to this stranger who had been his son. The city . . . It's *there* the days are the same. I thought it was very lonely in the city, the time I was there. The stone things move, but they do not change. My feet were always on stone. I could not walk on the ground and look over it and know it was my own. They never looked at the sky there, or listened for the rain.

When I looked at the sky there, the sun I saw was a strange one . . . it did not make friends with the stone. The stone houses were alike, and the days were alike, and never till they died could the people lie in bed at night and listen to rain on the corn after a long heat. They had nothing to breathe but their own tired breaths. I remember their faces. There was stone in them, too. They were all alike. They looked as if they never awoke from their tired dreams of the night. Their minds kept turning in their own tracks, like the weary wheels that could find no rest on the pavements. The soft-fingered, women-faced men lived in houses, and the house-smell clung to everything they said or did when they went outside. When they talked, it was empty, because their eyes saw nothing but the stone things that their hands had not built . . . and none of them had anything to say that could not be said with words. It was very lonely there. They laughed too much. But not even love or death could melt their aloneness. Even when they laughed, their eyes did not change. And when they died, no one remembered, and there was nothing left of them.

I liked it in the city, now, this time, David thought. The street lights began to come on, a little before it was dark, and excitement seemed to stir in the busy pavements. The wind was not strong enough to lift itself above the street, but the women's skirts clung to their bodies as they passed. So many different

144

women's bodies! What if they *didn't* speak? The bright, metallic faces of always-rich women seemed to shine in the shop-window light, and you knew you would feel clumsy and ashamed with them, but it was good to think of having their soft flesh alone somewhere in the dark. There was so much light there, then . . . and life. Like when you took off your work-clothes and shaved and felt smoother and brighter and ready for things. There was life, not death, at the end of the day. Here, my God . . . the same old bare maples weaving back and forth against a sky that made your lips blue just to look at it, and never the sound of a strange voice, and later the snow sifting lonely through the spokes of the wagon wheels . . . What a God-forsaken place to be *young* in. Maybe his father didn't mind, they didn't seem to mind *missing* things when they got old. Old people didn't seem to dread being quiet and letting things slip like this. They thought it was because they were wise . . . it was because they were half-dead already. If he thought he'd ever get like that about things when he got old . . . He'd never get old. He swore a desperate promise to himself that he'd never, never, never get that awful patience like his father . . . standing there now, with that stupid look on his face, like one of the oxen. . . .

"But Dave," Martin said slowly, "this place will be *yours* some day, you know that."

"What do *I* want of this old place?"

A whiteness came into Martin's face that was different from the whiteness of the cold or the weariness. He remembered the day his father had said the same thing to him. They had both felt shy and awkward, and he could say nothing, but as soon as he was alone, he had looked over this land, the tight tears of pride came warm into his eyes. He had kept this place, the best thing he had, till he could give it to his own son, and now when he offered it to David he saw it meant nothing. That he despised it. He had known through and through how his own father felt.

"It was always good enough here for *me*," Martin said.

"All right, but what did you ever *amount* to?"

145

Martin was stung into a sudden anger. "As much as *you* ever will, you..."

Then he looked over the fields, slowly, and a break came into his anger. Why today, only a few hours ago, starting to plow, it had been, without a thought, so sweet, so safe, so sure... he and his son plowing and him trying to show David how to turn the furrow better and David trying his best. Things just didn't come handy for David, it must be that. He had half felt Ellen working quiet and happy in the house and the smoke went straight from the chimney into the clear, sun-filled air and there had been no hurry or fret in the fields or the slow oxen or his thoughts. Now... it could never be the same again between him and David, now. Every time they said a sharp word to each other now, these sick things would all come back . . . What if David was right? What *had* he ever amounted to? Well, he had been young here, and youth was very fresh and full here in the fields and the sun and very long, some of it never died, it grew green again with each April sun. He had had a wife of his own kind, and everything they had, they had got with their own hands, his hands and hers. There had been a lot of tiredness but there was always the quiet night afterwards and the slow kindly talk. There had never been an end of work, but you could always stop to talk across the fields to your neighbour, and you got along just the same. There had not been much money, but there had always been the sweet smell of bread in the kitchen and the soft song of wood in the kitchen stove. There had been no strangers among them, and when you died these men you had lived your whole life with would not work that day, even if there was clover to be hauled in and rain in the wind... and you would lie in the land that your hands and your feet knew best, and the same breezes you had breathed would always blow over you. Surely that was enough for a man. If your son... If David ... It was hard to believe that your own son stayed on... It was hard to believe that your own son was not like you wanted him to be. But, Martin thought sadly, you couldn't make him see, if

146

he didn't feel that way. You wished . . . but if he felt that way, there was no way to make him see.

"Well Dave," Martin said slowly, "if you're *bound* to go away, I suppose . . ."

"Oh," David said impatiently, "let it go, let it go . . . I'll stay," he added sullenly.

He is almost afraid of me, Martin thought. He won't even talk it over with me. He has no use for my talk. He wants to keep me away from him. He don't think I can understand him at all. I try . . .

He walked around to the oxen's heads and picked up the whip.

"Haw," he said quietly. "Just cut her light here, son."

David put his hands back on the handles but he didn't speak. He threw the plow around when they turned the furrows, so the chain jerked taut in the yoke. "Easy now, boys," Martin cajoled the oxen.

A bare little wind started in the bare maples. The sun burned cold and lonesome in the blind windows of the church across the road and the long withered grass bent over the cold grey sand in the middle of the built-up graves. Peter's grave . . . Peter would coax to hold the whip. He could hardly make his small voice loud enough to stir the oxen, but they obeyed him. Martin could see the crazy nostrils of the running horses and then Peter's small crumpled body on the rock heap where the wheel had struck . . . .

The cows came up from the pasture, calling hollowly to be let in. The sky looked away from its own darkening face in the mud-bottomed puddles of the road. The blood in Martin's face came blue to the skin, and his blue eyes, a little faded with weariness, looked like frozen spots holding up the weight of his face. He walked back-to, guiding the oxen by the horns to help David keep the furrow straight, but David did not straighten his back, even when Martin stopped for a rock. Martin would come around and kick out the rock himself.

147

Martin blew on his hands and tried to start a smile in the corners of his tired, cold-thin, lips.

"Time for mittens, I guess. *Your* hands cold?"

"No," David said.

A shaft of the sun broke for a minute through the blue, wind-cold clouds. Long bands of it searchlit the grey rocks, without warming them.

"Snow comin'," Martin said.

The sun went down, and the sky made a few cold-pink patterns at the horizon. It would not be as sad again until April.

Martin turned the oxen for one more furrow. He could not stop, until he was *sure* how David ... Maybe if he kept on, David would say something himself about stopping, and he could show him then how ready he was to listen to him and take the oxen off the tongue.

"*I'll* never ask him to stop if he plows all night ..." David was so tired the muscles in his legs felt like a frayed rope and a tight cord drew his temples together. The blood seemed to drain from his face and throb heavy in his neck. The ashes of weariness sifted through the bright surface of his thoughts. The oxen lifted their heavy feet and deposited them carefully on the ground. The plow dug its slow way through the earth.

"I guess we're just gettin' her done in time," Martin said.

David said nothing.

"I guess this clears things up, about, for winter. You'll have a little more time to hunt, now, Dave."

Ellen came to the corner of the house, holding down her apron with one hand against the tug of the wind, and called supper.

"All right," Martin called back.

"Hungry, Dave?" he said.

"No."

David glanced at his father's face. For the first time he noticed how tired it looked. He felt sorry for his father, for a minute, and a little ashamed. He'd *have* to stay as long as his father was alive, he supposed.

They came to the end of the furrow. Martin hesitated.

"Well, I guess we'll let her go at that for tonight," he said. "We can wind her up in the morning, easy." He hesitated again.

"Dave," he said, "if you really *want* to go away..."

David's impatience flared again. He forgot his father's face.

"Oh, for God's sake," he said, "can't you let that *drop?* I said I'd say, didn't I? What more do you want? I'll stay here as long as *you're* here, anyway. So you need not worry."

So it is that way. A small coal touched suddenly against Martin's heart. He will wait, but he will be glad ... so he can go away. If he was waiting for it, so the place would be all his own then, it would be ... but he will be waiting, so he can go away. There will be a stranger here, and nothing will be done the same. There will be a strange name in my house, and maybe they will let the alders creep back over the acre field because they did not clear it for the first time and plow it with their own hands ... and the grass will grow tall and strange over the graves.

He pulled the bolt from the tongue. It was true. It was true, then. He *had* no son. David took his hands from the plow. Martin waited for a minute to see if he would line the plow up for the next furrow in the morning. David did not move. Martin walked around to the plow. David went to the oxen's head, took up the whip, and started with them to the barn. Martin pulled the plow around and lay the chain straight out along the next furrow. Ellen came to the corner of the house and called supper again, but Martin did not answer. He watched David take the oxen past the house. He saw Ellen say something to him, but David did not reply.

He bent down and dug the mud from the plowshare. It shone underneath, where the earth had polished it, like a sword. The earth smelled cold and silent. He moved a few stones, absently, with his foot and stood for a minute with his eyes on the ground. Like the night they buried Peter. He felt lost in the long, dead day.

In the porch, he listened to see if David might be talking to the oxen. There was no sound but the bells, as David jerked the yoke-straps. Martin caught his breath quickly. He *had* no son. Peter was dead. He *had* no son, now. He scraped the dirt from his heels with a stick from the chipyard and went inside the house.

"Well, what in the *world* have you two been doing?" Ellen said, moving across the scrubbed soft-wood floor from the stove to the table. The warm breath of food rose sweet in the oil-lamp-light. She held the dipper of water for Martin's hands over the basin in the sink. "Are you goin' to do a coupla more acres after supper?" she joked.

"Yeah, I was kinda thinkin' we might," Martin laughed.

But his laughter was heavy and grey, like a hawk rising.

Temptation

Alden Nowlan

The boy is
badgering the man
to lower him down the
face of the cliff
to a narrow shelf
about eight feet
below:
"Your hands are strong,
and I'm not afraid.
The ledge is wide enough,
I won't hurt myself
even if you let go."

"Don't be a fool.
You'd break every bone
in your body.
Where in God's name
do you get such ideas?
It's time we went home."

But there is no
conviction in the
man's voice and
the boy persists;
nagging his wrists,
dragging him nearer.
Their summer shirts
balloon in the wind.

While devils whisper
what god-like sport
it would be
to cling to the
edge of the world

and gamble
one's only son
against wind
and rocks
and sea.

He raids the refrigerator and reflects on parenthood

Alden Nowlan

Nowlan, you maudlin boob,
almost blubbering because
two hours ago at the party
your son said, I'll be
fifteen tomorrow, can I
have a whole pint of beer?
Grinning so he could say
it was a joke if you
took it that way; but he
was serious all right:
it's like music sometimes
how serious he can be
about small matters
which you're thereby
reminded were
important.
          And you hesitated,
not because you ever
considered refusing
but because you wanted him
to know that you, too,
value rituals. But
there were only enough
cool ones for the guests.
So you gave him a warm one.
It doesn't matter, he said.
It's okay. But of course it did.
The rite was spoiled
by an imperfection. And now he's
asleep upstairs and you're
holding open the door
of the refrigerator, contemplating
a pint bottle with no more

than two ounces taken from it
and the cap put back so well
you'd need an opener
to take it off again, thinking
of the petty treason
we commit so often
against those we love,
the confidence games
in which parents play
their children for suckers.

Loneliness of the long distance runner

Elizabeth Jones

"Loneliness of the long distance runner,"
Phrase burning, tingling and fading again
In the contracted furnace of my brain:
    "Loneliness
     Loneliness
     Loneliness of the long distance runner."

And no joyful fugue of a jazz trumpet
    Free and light
As the runner's footfalls,
    Light and free
As blobs of sunlight
    Bobbing about
On the path escaping
Beneath the poise of the feet,
Just blank walls
And the hard hospital bed
With its red waterproof sheet
Slightly slithering beneath
The heave and push
Of my clumsy body new to childbirth,
And the phrase
Glowing and burning
Branding itself on my brain:
"Loneliness of the long distance runner."

And when I held the child
    And knew it for mine,
I could not shout the race was done and won
Brandishing my trophy
For the world to admire,
For what I saw
In the tiny clenched fists
The eyes blind ahead

Was again my loneliness
The loneliness of the child
The loneliness of all long distance runners.

A Wonder of Wishes

H. R. Percy

That's something he gets from her: the way the blue eyes, after a moment of merry wistfulness, close so tight that the lashes almost vanish, only their extreme tips feathering golden from the dark thin frontier-line of eyelids. Creases shatter the smoothness even of his childish face. The sense of shattering finds echo within me. The lips, too, compress, upturning; the small nose crinkles and the cheeks, already rosy with the nip of December, blow and kindle with delight. The narrow shoulders lift a little and draw together, the arms hugging protectively the frail nursling of a newborn wish. The world of hard reality stands rebuked, seems ready to slink away ashamed, vanquished by so much fervour, so much faith.

Then he looks up at me, laughing, his eyes bright with the wonder of what he has seen, and pummels me with his mittened fists. Between us the mirthful billows of his breathing linger and fade. I swallow the gall of my guilty foreknowledge and smile down upon his plump face ringed in silvery fur. Off he goes, running. He runs with purpose, like one with a secret to share. Lost in my own reverie, I watch him with half an eye, dwindling down the long perspective of the pathway, dissolving into the mist that dusts the shrubberies with rime. Over the ghostly façade of the Lord Nelson a dazzle of sunlight seeps through, so

157

that all the trees sparkle like chandeliers and the ducks leave shimmering wakes on the ice-fringed water. An after-image of his wistfulness loiters in my mind's eye, and rendered unwary by the scene's frosty magic I let the image grow long hair the colour of the sun-soaked mist, and ear-rings that flash icy fire as they swing — Christmas-given in answer to her big-girl version of his little-boy wish. A might-have-been memory.

Standing in the slush before Birks' window, pressing her big belly to the sill, she ogles the ear-rings we can't possibly afford with a kid coming and goes into her little orgasm of covetous ecstasy. She turns to me breathless with it and says: "They're bee-oo-tiful." And on Christmas morning when I give her the gloves I suddenly see her standing there all aglow with wishing, the bright lights of Barrington Street strung out to infinity behind her like an invitation to adventure. But now her eyes have a different sparkle, which after the dutiful kiss she turns to hide, the hiccup she gets more often as the baby grows sounding very like a sob. The gloves are too small.

I harden against it, try to exorcise it by rekindling my old anger.

"Good God, woman. …!"

But all the old imperatives desert me now in my time of need. The new car smashed up and long forgotten. The fancy crib outgrown and given away. The avocado refrigerator now elegantly enshrining only beer and TV dinners. All so urgent once, so necessary: all such good excuses for a gift not given, a gesture not made, a wish denied. A stupidly sentimental thought hovers at the edge of my mind: I'd trade them all to have seen her in those ear-rings. To have made her truly happy. Once. Her face blissful between parentheses of fire. To have yielded just one to that occasional urge of hers to do something a little crazy, a little extravagant.

Well, to hell with her, anyway.

When I snap out of it there's no sign of him. No panic. But I quicken my pace a little. If he gets lost they'll never let him stay with me again. Couldn't believe my luck, getting him for Christmas. Searching for him I wonder why she agreed to it. Other plans. Plans that don't include a kid.

Now anger comes, fires my belly like a good belt of rum, gives me strength against the lure of sentiment.

"Seen a kid around? Blond hair? So big?"

The old guy pushes off from the parapet and turns to regard me blearily. He wags a crust of bread under my nose. Below, the ducks wait expectant. He sucks in his lips so that for a moment he is mouthless, the grey whiskers healing over the wound. I recognize him now. He delivers for Simpsons. Or is it Eaton's? Always screws up the orders.

He knows me, too. Always give him hell. But now he smiles and shakes his head: not in negation but amused at a memory. He's not very bright.

"Great little guy," he says at last, chuckling. "Great little guy." He jerks his thumb in the direction of the bandstand. Still wagging his head he tosses the last of the bread to the ducks and walks away, not very steadily.

"Gonnagettaboggan."

He grins up at me from the bandstand steps, where he sits swinging his feet, rocking his body back and forth.

"I don't think so, sport." We've been through it before. No place to use a toboggan where she lives. Nowhere to keep it. Et Cetera.

"Sanda said so."

"Big boys don't believe in Santa. That's for little kids."

Before, he pouted when I said it. Now, his grin broadens with man-to-man conspiracy.

"You're havin' me on."

"No, really, I. ..."

"Gotta wish big, Sanda said. Ever you want sumpin special, wish big."

We take the bus out to the shopping centre. He gazes out the window and chatters away, but every so often he goes very quiet and still, and glancing down I catch him wishing big. At Simpsons I leave him demolishing a Himalaya of ice cream while I slip out and order the giant dump truck. Battery operated. Power hoist. Every boy's dream. When I get back he is sliding little toboggans of wafer-biscuit down the smooth mountainside of his sundae.

"O.K., sport. Eat up."

He gives an eyes-bigger-than-belly sigh. On the long gentle slope of vanilla fudge I stand beside her as he comes hurtling down on his flying saucer and spreadeagles in the snow at our feet. Gorsebrook. Only last year.

"Why don't we get a toboggan?" she says. "One we can all ride on."

"Yeah," I say. "Why don't we?" My sneering tone drops the temperature another ten degrees. She snatches up the kid and rushes off. I hear him bawling while I pick up the flying saucer and send it sailing through the air into the bushes.

"Come on, leave that."

The sharp tone brings tears to his eyes. I wipe his face with a less-than-gentle hand.

The next day is Christmas Eve and dammit I have to work late shift. The neighbour's kid sits in. For an extortionate fee. I walk her home, both of us half asleep.

"Simpsons come?"

"Yeah. I left it with the janitor like you said till he went to sleep. Then I put it under the tree."

She's a pretty kid and I fight down a preposterous urge to kiss her goodnight. I go back, glance in on the kid and drop into bed exhausted. But for a long time I can't sleep.

"Gottaboggan! Gottaboggan!"

It takes me a while to surface. He is dragging a red and yellow toboggan round the floor, laughing, glowing, agog with shrill excitement. The sun streams in.

"No," I say. "There's some mistake. We'll have to take it back."

160

He doesn't hear me.

"Good old Sanda!"

"Blast his boozy eyes!" I see again the look of bleary cunning as he casts his meagre largesse upon the waters and slowly weaves away.

"Meddling old fool!"

"Who ya talkin' to, Dad?"

"Never mind. Go brush your teeth."

After breakfast he stands in the window, still holding the toboggan by its rope.

"Gee, I wish it would snow."

Ten minutes later, the dishes done, I find him still there. His eyes are tight shut and he is whispering. "Wish big. Wish big." There isn't a cloud in the sky. The earth is midsummer-bare.

By noon the snow is five inches deep. At two the sun comes out again. I submit to the inevitable, not with good grace. Just after two-thirty I am unloading the toboggan from the trunk of the car and he is dancing up and down in the snow shouting, "Oh, boy! Oh, boy! Oh, boy!"

We're the first on the slopes. We take a couple of runs down, leaving long snaking scars on the unsullied whiteness. The third time we take a tumble and he rolls shrieking with laughter in the snow. I laugh in spite of myself. Then I let myself go. What the hell! Again and again we trudge up, hurtle down, his arms tight about me, his hot breath upon my neck.

Halfway up we stop for breath. Others have arrived now. They shoot by, girls squealing, clinging.

"Gee, Dad, wouldn't it be great if...?"

I find my mind wandering as we stand there trumpetting breath.

"Yeah," I say without thinking. "Wouldn't it be great."

When I come to with a start he is just opening his eyes and I know he has been wishing very, very big.

161

Professor Out Of Work
in memory of my father Kenneth Thurston

Harry Thurston

I

My education in disuse
I laboured,
tried to teach the five-thumbed hands
to plumb
   plane
   level.
At night
the gable's angle
cut at my eyes—
the slip
hammer blow
of flesh/blood
cleaved.
In a hospital bed
his body lay beyond repair,
A house no carpenter
(however skillful)
could cure.

II

The freedom of taking up one's bed
denied
   (the body's betrayal)
place exerts its tyranny.

I came to the hospital
as an envoi
bearing a reprieve
to one in exile.
I wanted to know,

would he find it too lonely
if he returned home?

His reply: *All I ever needed*
was a book
and a window.

III

Always at the day's first meal
an open book
    face down
marked his place.
Now when I find myself
imitating his trick,
pages paperweighted
with a table knife,
his face rises up,
for too long now
the mask of his sickness—
when in health
he returned sawdust
in cuff and collar
    (eagerly
out of overalls into dustjackets)
devoured novels
    held farsightedly
below bifocals.
Always a man of few words
but well chosen:
The day a man
puts on overalls
he might as well
forget it.
    Pronounced like
    a life sentence.

IV

Baker
Farmer
Cabinetmaker:
All of them acts

(white scarf,
black great coat,
postures in the family album
the same as the dandies
swaggering out of the roaring 20s
celluloid)

A professor out of work,
that's what I looked like,
said the self-effacing farmer
(eyes set ironically
in rimless hexagons).
And we laughed
knowing it to be true.

my brother

Sharon Lake

my brother walks
the roads,
his hands deep
in his jean pockets,
his feet bouncing
in his sneakers

      probably borrowed on the run.

he walks
the mile to town,
to sit on the cold hard
steps of the telephone office.

perhaps he meets
a friend,
perhaps
the rain forces him
into a waiting car

      gunning its motor
      impatient to travel
      anywhere the streets go.

perhaps
he sits alone
till the lights
go on over the empty stores,
till its dark
enough to come home.

Jimmie Machum

Gregory M. Cook

Jimmie Machum worked his own ground
no thanks to anyone.
Slaughtered beef and pork single-handed
except the wife
she poured scalding water.
"Live alone. Work alone. And leave alone."

Jimmie Machum was never seen off his farm.
Some said he'd lost his license driving drunk.
Jimmie said he didn't need it.
"The wife can drive. And the kids go praying."

The August of his best crops
Jimmie Machum was seen digging in the graveyard.
In separate boxes from his own woodlot
went twin sons two months too early,
one still-born, the other dead in four days.
Jimmie Machum worked his own ground.

Requiescam

When I am laid out
amid the gaudy glories of Kelly's Funeral Parlour,
with the electric crucifix
and the bloodless landscapes on the wall,
(while the next corpse waits in the back room)
don't surround me
with fat blossoms from a flower shop,
but rather
get my children and grandchildren to gather
bunches of weedy wildflowers,
mayflowers, pink orchids from the swamp, black-eyed susies,
whatever's in season,
Even, if it s the dead of winter,
some clubmoss or a patch of red lichen
then, perhaps, my friends will recognise me
and, having felt some pang of regret,
will remove their sober faces
and hold a party in my remembrance.

Hurt

Alden Nowlan

When I grow up there ain't nothin' ever gonna hurt me. Not ever," Stevie used to tell me, doubling up his grimy fists until his knuckles whitened, and snarling like a small, trapped animal, a fox or a feral cat maybe, as he squeezed back the tears at the corners of the eyes that looked ridiculously huge in his peaked ten-year-old's face.

He'd say that after the health nurse sent him home from school because there were lice in his whiskey-coloured mop of hair again or after one of the kids teased him about his old man getting drunk and losing his job at the mill for probably the tenth time that summer, and maybe after Mom or somebody tried to give him a second-hand polo shirt.

The only plans I'd made for growing up were that I was going to be a cowboy, a locomotive engineer, a pirate and maybe pitcher for the Brooklyn Dodgers. Stevie lived in a trailer across the bridge from our farm. I thought it must be wonderful to live in a trailer and not have somebody yelling at you all the time to take off your rubbers when you came into the house.

Stevie's old man yelled at him plenty but only when he was drunk. When he was sober he let him do whatever he liked. Stevie went to school when he wanted to go and when he was bored with it he stayed home or spent the day on the marsh or in

168

the woods. He fixed his own meals and sometimes ate six chocolate bars and a bottle of pop for supper.

Stevie wasn't like any of the other kids who came to school
in dirty sweat shirts and were sent home lousy. There were a
dozen kids in Hastings Mills public school like that. Muscular
thirteen-year-olds spending their fifth year in Grade V, knowing
that next year they'd be free to chuck their exercise books and
get a job on somebody's farm or at the mill. Wet-nosed little
girls who wore wrinkled dresses that almost tickled their ankles
and stole everything from the Junior Red Cross treasury to the
buttons on the teacher's coat. Stevie never studied and he was
usually at the head of the class. When he wasn't in first place it
was because he'd stayed home the week we had exams, lying on
his belly in the grass in front of the trailer reading a book old
man Simms had given him, or picking lady's slippers in the
swamp or building the biggest kite we'd ever seen, or something
like that. Old man Simms was supposed to be crazy and rich.
Eventually he was buried by the parish. Every Hallowe'en he
patrolled his farm with a shotgun loaded with rock salt. Natural-
ly, stealing his mail box was the finest adventure of the year. He
liked Stevie and gave him a book called *The Boy's Book of
Heroes*, all about people like Xerxes and Xenophon and Achilles
and Napoleon. Stevie read it all that summer we were ten. When
I went over to the trailer after school or on Saturdays and suggested we play war, I always wanted to fight Nazis and Japs but
Stevie wouldn't play unless we fought Persians or Trojans.

The more Trojans we killed in the games the better Stevie
liked it. We picked cat-tails in the swamp, dried them in the sun
and used them as torches when we razed Troy. Stevie sprinkled
half a box of salt on the burnt grass and said that's what you
were supposed to do when you conquered a city because then
"there won't never be anything grow there anymore." At the end
I always had to be Hector and he was Achilles and killed me
with a wooden sword. He swung the sword with furious intensi-
ty, forcing me to back away from him. His teeth clenched and

his eyes were slits in his white face. He was quick as a cat and sometimes sharp smacks from the sword on my arms and chest goaded me into bringing my stave down on his shoulder or wrist with all my strength and anger behind the blow so that it left a red blotch that gradually turned blue wherever it hit. After hitting him I was always ashamed. But he'd say, "That's the way, Skip, that's the way to do it," and keep boring in until we agreed that I was dead and went swimming.

Stevie couldn't bear to see real things die. My brother Chuck let us go out with him to try out a new .22 and Stevie liked watching him shoot holes through a tomato can and knock chips off the fence posts but when he sent a squirrel spinning out of a tree and we walked over and looked down at the little limp bundle of fur and blood, Stevie's lips were shivering as if someone had dropped an icicle down the neck of his shirt and his eyes looked exactly like those of a fawn the dogs killed one winter in the field back of our house.

"Why did you have to kill it?" he said and Chuck looked down at him, not knowing what to say, and Stevie started crying, pressing his palms into his eyes.

The winter after that, he found all of Bill Taylor's rabbit snares and stole them.

Sometimes when I went over to the trailer, Stevie's old man was drunk on moonshine or homebrew or vanilla extract. One Saturday he'd be lying on the sofa with his shirt and boots off, singing at the top of his voice and ending each verse with an explosion of laughter. Then next Saturday he'd be pounding the walls with his fists and swearing and crying at the same time or maybe lying on the floor or in the grass, snoring and mumbling in his sleep, waking up every little while to vomit.

When he was happy-drunk and wanted to sing he gave Stevie cigarettes. When it was summer we sat on the ground behind the trailer, with our bare knees drawn up under our chins, and smoked, with Stevie inhaling like a man and me just letting the cigarette burn down as I held it in my mouth. Stevie had no "respect" for his old man, not the kind of respect Pop was always telling me I was supposed to have for him, but when he passed out and started shivering Stevie threw a coat over his shoulders. And Sunday mornings when the old man was too sick to go himself, Stevie went down to the store and got him a couple of bottles of vanilla to sober up on.

Sometimes I met him on my way to Sunday School, me itching and sweating in my starched shirt and my toes aching in leather shoes. He'd be barefoot and wearing a pair of dirty denim shorts. He'd have the vanilla bottles in a paper bag and maybe be carrying something crazy like a big bouquet of daisies in the other hand. Once or twice I went back to the trailer with him and after the old man drank the vanilla he'd give us whatever change he had in his pockets and we'd go back to the store and buy some chocolate bars with old Mason, the storekeeper, teasing me about what Pop would do to me if he found out about me running around with Stevie when I was supposed to be in Sunday School, and then short-changing us because he knew I wouldn't dare tell. Stevie wasn't afraid to tell, but he ignored it. He took it for granted that people were going to cheat him every chance they got.

Then we'd go swimming in the creek and I'd feel free and fine, pulling my torturing Sunday clothes off and feeling the soreness ooze out of my feet when we ran across the cool mud toward the water. One Sunday on the creek bank Stevie tried to teach me to play cards, giving me half his money and then manipulating the pieces of greasy pasteboard until he'd won it all back.

He didn't laugh when he won. Stevie seldom laughed at anything. When he smiled it wasn't a kid's grin. I thought it was like Mom smiled sometimes when you weren't quite sure she was smiling at you or at anything you could see but maybe at something inside her you couldn't understand, something that was even a little sad. Stevie found a duck with a broken leg and made it a splint out of a shingle and kept it in a box in the trail-

171

er, trying to get it to eat bread crumbs, and after a week it died. When he knelt down to coax it to eat he always had that funny, sad little smile.

When he did laugh his whole body vibrated with it and he'd roll on the ground, hugging himself and laughing, until tears ran down his cheeks and he blew his nose and rocked back and forth, trying to get his breath. His laughter always scared me a little and I'd punch him in the chest and yell at him and once I threw a dipperful of cold water in his face and he only laughed harder.

When Stevie cried it was never for the reasons the rest of the kids cried. Miss Grant, who taught school at Hastings Mills the year I was ten, strapped him every time he skipped school and while she was smacking him he bit his lower lip and blinked at the blackboard and after it was over he went back to his desk and spat on his palms and thumbed his nose at her elaborately as she turned her back, so that everyone laughed.

But one noon hour when he had nothing for lunch except a gooey chocolate bar and she offered him some of her sandwiches, he bolted away from her and afterwards I found him in the woodshed, lying face down in the sawdust, his shoulders shaking with sobs.

That was one of the times that he told me when he grew up nothing was ever going to hurt him.

"When I grow up, Skip, there ain't nothin' ever gonna hurt me," he said. But he didn't stop crying.

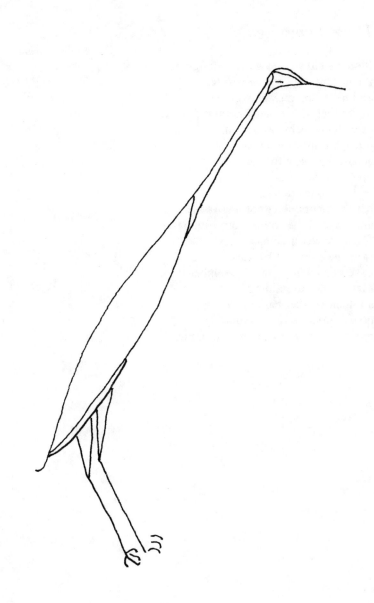

Heron

Long, Long, Ago

Alden Nowlan

It seems I always saw the Indian woman
the instant she became visible,
and never took my eyes off her
as she lugged her many-coloured pack,
three times as big as herself,
down South Mountain,
across the Little Bridge,
up North Mountain
and into our kitchen
where she undid a knot
and flooded the entire room with baskets
—cherry-coloured baskets,
cabbage-coloured baskets,
baskets the colour of a November sky,
each basket containing
another, smaller basket,
down to one so tiny it would hold
only a hang of thread and a thimble.

We make baskets

Rita Joe

We make baskets of ash and maple,
Good wood.
Intricate designs, carefully woven,
nothing crude,
Perfection binding.

Women of peace,
We weave each day.

Poet, Weaver, Woman, Dreamer

Maxine Tynes

sometimes
as I sit weaving
words flow
much as the fibre flows through my fingers
with colour and texture
finely tuned, like the tension of
my ancient tapestry
this craft of some long-ago brown Aztec woman
reborn in my hands
confuses itself with the poet-woman I am
and the words come through
not to be written
but to web themselves into the fabric
                              into the colour
and fibre of my work.

perhaps in the long-ago lifetime
of that brown Aztec woman
I was the spider-woman high on her mud ceiling
with jealous spider-web eyes on her craft
the webbing, the weaving of her 'God's Eyes'
and now, in this life
as a poet-woman and weaver
the 'God's Eyes' are mine to make
and, feeling the words coming, too
I wonder, who is casting jealous eyes on me.

Poem After Months

Sparling Mills

How do others live
Without poetry?
Action is fine,
Until strength collapses for the day.
We all come to the thought-times,
The aloneness of an empty house,
The fear that nothing we do
Really matters.

How do others fill emptiness,
If not with the tantalizing bubble
Of possible creation?

I have lived months without the stirrings
Of line rhythms;
Months I would not re-live for
Anything material.

Now, I am impressed
With the courage of men and women
Who find fulfillment in everyday affairs.
But I am one of the weak ones.
I must have the intoxicating goal
Of possible perfection;
I must live life in expectation of a poem,
The poem,
Which is always the next.

BIOGRAPHICAL NOTES

(Elizabeth) Joan Balcom, a native of the Annapolis Valley, now lives in Berwick. She has been a journalist and freelance magazine writer for over twenty years. Two of her publications, *The Mystic East and Fundy Tales,* recount legends that originated along the Bay of Fundy Coast.

Will R. Bird (1891) Born in East Mapleton, N.S., he served in World War I and has written about his war experiences. Bird is perhaps best known for his tales of the Yorkshiremen in Cumberland County. He has received several literary awards; some of his best known writings are *Sunrise for Peter, This is Nova Scotia*, and *The Two Jacks.*

Charles Bruce (1906-1971) was born in Port Shoreham, N.S. He worked for the Canadian Press for many years, becoming London Superintendent during World War II, and in 1945 head of CP. Bruce published two novels, *The Channel Shore* and *The Township of Time*, and a number of books of poetry. One of the best known of these is *The Mulgrave Shore.*

Ernest Buckler (1908) was born at Dalhousie West in the Annapolis Valley. He attended Dalhousie University and the Universtiy of Toronto. For much of his life he has lived on his farm near Bridgetown. Buckler's *The Mountain and the Valley* is generally regarded as one of the best novels written in Canada. He has also written, *The Cruelest Month, Rebellion of Young David and other Stories, Ox Bells and Fireflies, Whirligig* and *Nova Scotia: Window on the Sea* (with Hans Weber). Buckler is noted for his sensitive portrayal of rural and family life.

Silver Donald Cameron (1937) lives in D'Escousse, N.S. He was a professor at U.N.B. and founding editor of *The Mysterious East* magazine. For several years he has been a free-lance journalist and broadcaster. Among his books are *Conversations with Canadian Novelists, Faces of Leacock*, and *The Education of Everett Richardson*.

Gregory M. Cook (1942), born in Yarmouth, now lives near Wolfville. He was a lecturer in the English Department at Acadia University until he began writing full-time. He writes poetry, short stories, plays, literary reviews and criticism. His work has appeared in many magazines and on the CBC.

Terry Crawford (1945) was born in Saint John, N.B. and now lives in the Annapolis Valley. His poetry has been published widely in literary magazines. Three of his books are *Lost Neighbourhood, Sorcerers Cafe*, and *The Werewolf Miracles*.

Dr. Helen Creighton (1899) was born in Dartmouth and still resides there. In 1929 she began collecting Nova Scotian ballads and folksongs; this activity expanded to include folklore, ghost stories and legends. Dr. Creighton is recognized as one of the foremost authorities in this field. Her books include *Songs and Ballads from Nova Scotia, Bluenose Ghosts*, and *Bluenose Magic*. Without her efforts a major part of our Maritime heritage would have been lost.

Frank Parker Day (1881–1950) was born in Shubenacadie and died near Yarmouth. He attended Pictou Academy, Mount Allison University, and Oxford as a Rhodes Scholar. Day taught in several American universities and was President of Union College. His novels, *River of Strangers, Rockbound*, and *John Paul's Rock,* did not receive much attention in Canada. *Rockbound* (reprinted in 1973) depicts the harsh and isolated life of outport fishermen in the early 20th century.

Thomas Chandler Haliburton (1796–1865) was born in Windsor. He was a lawyer, member of the legislative assembly, and finally a judge. In 1856 he went to England and became a member of the British House of Commons. Stephen Leacock and Haliburton are regarded as the foremost Canadian humorists and satirists. His creation, Sam Slick, first appeared in Joseph Howe's newspaper, *The Novascotian*. Eventually Haliburton wrote three books, *The Clockmaker*, *Sam Slick's Wise Saws* and *Nature and Human Nature*. They achieved immense popularity in Europe and North America.

Chipman Hall (1941) was born in Halifax. He has worked with the CBC and Canadian Press. His first novel, *Lightly*, won first prize in the Nova Scotia Writers Federation novel competition.

Bill Howell (1946) was born in England and grew up in Halifax. His poems have appeared in many magazines and in his book, *The Red Fox*. Howell has written for radio and television and works for the CBC.

Rita Joe (1931) was born in Whycocomagh, Nova Scotia, and now lives at East Bay, Eskasoni Reserve. Many of her poems and records of Micmac legends have been published in the *Micmac News* and, most recently, in *Bluenose Magazine*.

Sharon Lake (1952) was born near Wolfville. After attending Acadia University, she travelled extensively in Europe and the U.S. She now lives and writes in Wolfville Ridge.

Kenneth Leslie (1892–1974) was born in Pictou. He studied at several universities including Dalhousie and Harvard. Leslie spent some time in the United States, returning to Halifax in later years. One of his books of poetry, *By Stubborn Stars*, won the Governor General's Award in 1938.

Donald Linehan was born in Singapore, raised in Ireland, has been a Nova Scotian Canadian for the last twenty-one years, and is an "Irish" English teacher. Living on the banks of the LaHave River, his poetry writing has become more prolific in the past six years; in 1977, he won first prize in the Nova Scotia Writers Federation competition.

Hugh MacLennan (1907) was born in Glace Bay. He was a Rhodes Scholar and Guggenheim Fellow. For many years he has been a professor at McGill University. MacLennan has won the Governor General's Award for Fiction three times and the Award for Non-fiction twice. Among his best known works are *Barometer Rising, Each Man's Son, Two Solitudes* and *The Watch That Ends the Night*.

Alistair MacLeod was born in Saskatchewan but was brought up mainly in Dunvegan and Inverness, Cape Breton. He studied at St. Francis Xavier, UNB and Notre Dame. He teaches literature and creative writing at the University of Windsor. His book of short stories, *The Last Salt Gift of Blood*, is a sensitive and subtle portrayal of life in Cape Breton.

Sparling Mills was born in Windsor, Ont. She now lives in Herring Cove, having also spent some time in South Africa and California. In addition to two books of poetry, *Woman, Be Honest* and *Falling in Love Again*, her work has been published in many literary magazines.

Alden Nowlan (1933) was born in Stanley, Hants Co. He lives in Fredericton where he has been writer-in-residence at U.N.B. since 1968. Nowlan is one of Canada's most respected poets; one of his many books of poetry, *Bread, Wine and Salt*, won the Governor General's Award in 1967. But he has also published a novel, *Various Persons Named Kevin O'Brien*; short stories, *Miracle at Indian River*; plays performed by Theatre New Brunswick, and many newspaper and magazine articles.

H. R. (Bill) Percy (1920) Born in England, Percy came to Canada in 1952. He spent many years in the British and Canadian navies and now lives in Granville Ferry. His short stories have appeared in several publications (including his book, *The Timeless Island*) and he has published a biography of Joseph Howe.

Susan Perly, from Dominion, Nova Scotia, works for the CBC. She has worked for Neptune Theatre in Halifax and wrote *Women and the Law in Nova Scotia.*

Thomas Raddall (1903) came to Canada from England in 1913. For five years he was a wireless operator. Since then, he has lived in Liverpool, working first as an accountant, and, from 1938, as a full-time writer. His novels have won three Governor General's Awards. Raddall's work has been translated into several languages. Thus, he has both a national and international reputation as a writer of fiction and historical works. Some of his best known works are *The Nymph and the Lamp*; *Halifax, Warden of the North*; *Roger Sudden* and *The Governor's Lady.*

Peter Sanger (1943) was born in Worcestershire, England, and came to Canada in 1952. He studied in Ontario and Australia and has taught in several Canadian universities. He is now assistant professor of English at the Nova Scotia Agricultural College. His poems were broadcast on CBC Anthology and have been published in several literary magazines.

Joseph Sherman (1945) was born in Bridgewater and grew up in Cape Breton. He now teaches English at College St. Louis-Maillet in Edmunston, N.B. His poetry has been published in several anthologies and magazines; he has written two books: *Birthday* and *Chaim the Slaughterer.*

Fraser Sutherland (1946) was born in Pictou. He was co-founder of *Northern Journey*, a literary magazine. His books of poetry are *Strange Ironies, Within the Wound* and *Madwoman,* soon to be published. He has also written a critical work, *The Style of Innocence, a Study of Hemingway and Callaghan*.

Harry Thurston (1950) was born in Yarmouth. He attended Acadia University and now lives in River Hebert, Cumberland County. He edits *Germination*, a poetry quarterly, and has had poetry published in several anthologies.

Maxine Tynes (1950), from Dartmouth, Nova Scotia, is an English teacher and very proud of her black heritage. Her poetry won an award in the 1977 Nova Scotia Writers' Federation competition and has appeared in *Herstory*, Saskatchewan Woman's Calendar.

PERMISSIONS

1. By permission from Joan Balcom for 'Jerome' from *The Mystic East*, G. R. Saunders, Ltd. 1972.

2. By permission from W. R. Bird for 'Paid-up Member' from *Sunrise for Peter, and Other Stories*.

3. By permission from Macmillan Company of Canada for 'Biography' and 'Girls in the Parlour' from *The Mulgrave Road*, 1951, Charles Bruce.

4. From *Window on the Sea* and *Rebellion of Young David and other Stories* by Ernest Buckler, reprinted by permission of the Canadian Publishers, McClelland and Stewart, Toronto.

5. By permission from Silver Donald Cameron for excerpt from *The Education of Everett Richardson*, 1977. Originally published by McClelland & Stewart, Toronto.

6. By permission from Gregory Cook for 'The Gods War Over a Golden Apple and Troy Falls All Over Again' and 'Jimmy Machum' (earlier draft published by *Alpha* 2:4, 1977.)

7. By permission from Terry Crawford for 'Barometer Descending' from *Sorcerers Cafe*, The Athanaeum, 1971.

8. By permission from Dr. Helen Creighton for 'George Jones' and 'Tangier Gold Mine' from *Songs and Ballads from Nova Scotia*, Dover Publications, New York, 1966.

9. By permission from Donald F. Day for Frank Parker Day, excerpt from *Rockbound*, University of Toronto Press, 1973.

10. By permission from Clarke-Irwin Canada to reprint excerpt from *Sam Slick Anthology*, 1969, Thomas Chandler Haliburton.

11. From *Lightly* by Chipman Hall reprinted by permission of the Canadian Publishers, McClelland and Stewart, Toronto.

12. From *The Red Fox* by Bill Howell, 'Seventeen Forty-Nine' and 'Sailmaker' by permission of the Canadian Publishers, McClelland and Stewart, Toronto.

13. By permission from Rita Joe and Abanaki Press for 'We Make Baskets' and 'Aye! No Monuments' from *Poems of Rita Joe*, Abanaki Press, Halifax, 1978.

14. By permission from Sharon Lake for 'my brother'.

15. By permission of Rosaleen Dickson for Kenneth Leslie's 'Halibut Cove Harvest'.

16. By permission from Thomas D. Linehan for 'Requiescam'.

17. By permission from Hugh MacLennan and Macmillan Company of Canada for excerpt from *Each Man's Son*.

18. From *The Last Salt Gift of Blood*, 'The Return' by Alistair McLeod by permission of the Canadian Publishers. McClelland and Stewart, Toronto.

19. By permission from Elizabeth Jones for 'Loneliness of the long distance runner' from *Castings*, Fiddlehead Press, 1972.

20. By permission of Nova Scotia Museum for *Rock Drawings of the Micmac Indians*.

21. By permission of Sparling Mills for 'Poem After Months', first published in *Woman, Be Honest*, 1974, reprinted 1976.

22. By permission from Clarke Irwin and Company Ltd. to reprint by Alden Nowlan: 'Temptation' (from *Bread Wine and Salt*, 1967), 'The Red Wool Shirt' (from *Smoked Glass*, 1977), 'The Mosherville Road' (from *The Mysterious Naked Man*, 1969), 'He Raids the Refrigerator and Reflects . . .' (from *Between Laughter and Tears*, 1971), 'Long, Long Ago' (from *Bread Wine and Salt*, 1967), 'Hurt' (from *Miracle at Indian River*, 1968).

23. By permission from H. R. Percy, 'A Wonder of Wishes' first published in *The Nova Scotia Times*, Nova Scotia Communications and Information Centre, 1975.

24. By permission of Susan Perly for 'The Land', first published in *Voices Down East*, 2.

25. By permission of Thomas H. Raddall for 'Winter's Tale'.

26. By permission of Peter Sanger, for 'Transit West'.

27. By permission of Joseph Sherman and Oberon Press for 'The Amazing Cannon at Liverpool, N.S.', from *Chaim the Slaughterer*, 1974.

28. By permission of Fraser Sutherland for 'Old N.S.' first published in *New: American and Canadian Poetry*.

29. By permission: Harry Thurston for 'Professor Out of Work, in Memory of My Father'.

30. By permission: Maxine Tynes for 'Poet, Weaver, Woman, Dreamer'.

31. BALLAD OF SPRINGHILL. By Ewan MacColl and Peggy Seeger. © Copyright 1960 by Stormking Music Inc. All rights reserved. Used by permission.

Acknowledgements

The editors wish to thank Jane Trimble, Sara MacRae and Hugh Rathbun for their advice and assistance.